Three Religious Leaders: Jesus, Buddha, and Muhammad

by Alan Moore & Gill Tavner / R.N. Pillai / Ahmed Abo Knegar

Level 2
(1300-word)

IBC パブリッシング

はじめに

　ラダーシリーズは、「はしご (ladder)」を使って一歩一歩上を目指すように、学習者の実力に合わせ、無理なくステップアップできるよう開発された英文リーダーのシリーズです。

　リーディング力をつけるためには、繰り返したくさん読むこと、いわゆる「多読」がもっとも効果的な学習法であると言われています。多読では、「1. 速く　2. 訳さず英語のまま　3. なるべく辞書を使わず」に読むことが大切です。スピードを計るなど、速く読むよう心がけましょう（たとえば TOEIC® テストの音声スピードはおよそ 1 分間に 150 語です）。そして 1 語ずつ訳すのではなく、英語を英語のまま理解するくせをつけるようにします。こうして読み続けるうちに語感がついてきて、だんだんと英語が理解できるようになるのです。まずは、ラダーシリーズの中からあなたのレベルに合った本を選び、少しずつ英文に慣れ親しんでください。たくさんの本を手にとるうちに、英文書がすらすら読めるようになってくるはずです。

《本シリーズの特徴》

- 中学校レベルから中級者レベルまで5段階に分かれています。自分に合ったレベルからスタートしてください。
- クラシックから現代文学、ノンフィクション、ビジネスと幅広いジャンルを扱っています。あなたの興味に合わせてタイトルを選べます。
- 巻末のワードリストで、いつでもどこでも単語の意味を確認できます。レベル1、2では、文中の全ての単語が、レベル3以上は中学校レベル外の単語が掲載されています。
- カバーにヘッドホーンマークのついているタイトルは、オーディオ・サポートがあります。ウェブから購入／ダウンロードし、リスニング教材としても併用できます。

《使用語彙について》

レベル1：中学校で学習する単語約1000語

レベル2：レベル1の単語＋使用頻度の高い単語約300語

レベル3：レベル1の単語＋使用頻度の高い単語約600語

レベル4：レベル1の単語＋使用頻度の高い単語約1000語

レベル5：語彙制限なし

Contents

Jesus of Nazareth

Alan Moore & Gill Tavner

【主な登場人物、地名など】

Nazareth ナザレ《地名》

John the Baptist 洗礼者ヨハネ《預言者》

Joseph ヨセフ《マリアの夫、イエスの養父》

Mary マリア《イエスの母》

Elizabeth エリサベト《洗礼者ヨハネの母》

Galilee ガリラヤ《地名》

River Jordan ヨルダン川

Sea of Galilee ガリラヤ湖

Bethsaida ベツサイダ《町の名》

Andrew アンデレ《十二使徒の一人》

Simon シモン《十二使徒の一人。のちのシモン・ペトロ》

Capernaum カファルナウム《町の名》

Mary Magdalene マグダラのマリア《人名》

Moses モーセ《古代イスラエルの民族指導者》

Judas Iscariot イスカリオテのユダ《十二使徒の一人》

Jairus ヤイロ《カファルナウムの会堂長》

King Herod ヘロデ大王《ユダヤ王国を統治した王》

Gennesaret ゲネサレト《地名》

Pharisee パリサイ（派の）人《保守的なユダヤ教の一派》

Elijah エリヤ《古代イスラエル民族の預言者》

Bethany ベタニア《地名》

Passover 過越《ユダヤ教の祭日の一つ》

Mount of Olives オリーブ山

Gethsemane ゲッセマネ《地名》

Pontius Pilate ポンテオ・ピラト《ユダヤ属州総督》

Golgotha ゴルゴタ《エルサレム付近の丘》

It wasn't until Jesus of Nazareth went to see John the Baptist that he fully understood what his work was to be.

His life in Nazareth as a child was a happy one. He had friends, loving brothers and sisters and, of course, his mother and Joseph. His parents told him wonderful stories about his earliest days; he listened with interest as their experiences became part of who he was.

As Jesus grew older, Joseph taught his son about his work making things out of wood. "You'll need to earn a living one day," he said.

Mary and Joseph were good Jews, following all the rules and teaching Jesus the scriptures. The more he studied, the more interested he became. "I *need* to study and pray," he tried to explain to his mother. "I feel that I have an important job to do, even more important than Joseph's work."

Mary looked worried, but not surprised.

As Jesus got older, his sense of purpose got stronger. All around him, people were making others' lives difficult. Those in the most need of kindness, the sick and the poor, were often treated the worst. Some religious leaders created even more problems by following the rules but not thinking about the needs of others, or by taking money from the poor. This couldn't be God's plan. Somebody needed to do something about these things.

Jesus was still living at home when, just before his thirtieth birthday, a relative called Elizabeth visited his family. She was worried about her son. "People call him John the Baptist," she smiled. "He's living south of Galilee, baptizing people in the River Jordan."

Jews like Jesus and his family were used to this, but John was also telling people to change the way they lived, just as the prophets of long ago had taught. "He says that he's preparing the way for somebody greater than him," Elizabeth told Jesus, "somebody who will baptize us with the Holy Spirit and with fire."

Jesus's mother looked at him. He saw how sad her eyes were as she quietly said, "You should visit him."

Jesus decided to walk the dusty miles to the River Jordan, where he found John.

"I've come to be baptized," Jesus said.

"I've been expecting you," John said to Jesus, "but surely it is *you* who should be baptizing *me*." Jesus didn't understand what he meant.

As John baptized him in the cold river, Jesus felt a surprising warm feeling in his heart. He suddenly saw God's love in everything in the world, and his heart was filled with love for everything.

As he came up out of the water, the heavens opened to Jesus, and he heard a loud voice from the sky saying, "You are my son, with whom I am well pleased!"

Jesus knew then that he was the man for whom John had been preparing the people. He was God's son. This was what he had been getting ready for all his life.

The joy that Jesus felt soon changed into fear and doubt. The Son of God? What could that mean? What kind of things would he have to do? Sons usually continued their father's work. As Joseph's son, Jesus had continued making things from wood. His job now was to do God's work on earth.

Needing to be alone, Jesus walked away from the river and into the desert. He stayed in that place for many weeks, praying to God, asking what his father wanted him to do.

He had come without any food, and soon Jesus grew hungry. An evil voice, which seemed to come from outside him, told Jesus that as the Son of God he had enough power to turn the stones around him into food.

"Go on — try it," said the voice.

Though he very much wanted to, Jesus knew this would be the wrong use of his power. He needed to pray, not think about food. He stopped worrying about feeling hungry, and the voice stopped talking to him.

So how *did* God want Jesus to use his power? What could he do?

The voice returned. "Hey, Son of God, throw yourself from this cliff. You'll be fine — God will save you."

"I already trust God. I don't need to test him."

"Then show the people how much power God has," said the voice. "Be a king."

"No!" Jesus shouted. "No! People cannot be forced to love God!" The voice stopped speaking.

There was only one way to do God's work. Jesus had to give up everything. He had to be modest, and he could not be selfish. He had to work hard to show people how to love God, and how to be good to each other. Whatever

7

it might take, Jesus had to make it possible for them to know — and to reach — God. Although he was afraid of where this might lead him, Jesus knew that God would give him the help he needed.

He had been given a simple but very difficult task. Leaving the desert, Jesus walked for days towards the Sea of Galilee. Looking around him, he was pained more than ever by all of the evil things in the world. People thought that wealth was a blessing from God, and, afraid of being poor, they wanted to keep everything that they had for themselves rather than sharing.

It wasn't only the poor who were having a hard time. No one wanted to be around sick people, so they had to leave their villages and their families.

In one town Jesus saw a sick man lying on the ground, his skin covered with sores. Although he was asking for food, everybody walked straight past him. Jesus had to act.

Jesus said to the people who were walking by, "Why aren't you helping this poor man?"

One man looked at Jesus. "Please give him some food," he said.

The man seemed nervous, but he came over to where Jesus and the beggar were. Touching the sick man, Jesus felt God's power pass through him. "Your sins are forgiven," Jesus said. He knew that God had given him the power to forgive sin, but it must have been a strange thing to hear.

Shaking, the beggar stood up. His sores began to heal. Jesus, too, was shaking. Both men looked at him.

"How can you forgive the bad things that people have done?" said the man who had been sick. "Only God can do that."

Jesus did not answer the question. He turned to the other man. "Feed him as you would want to be fed if you were hungry."

"Yes," he replied. "I will."

God had given Jesus his love and also the power to change people's lives, as well as asking Jesus to bring people back to him. He continued to travel around Galilee, healing people and telling them how important it was to love each other.

Although Jesus's message was simple, many did not understand it well. As word spread about his work, the crowds grew larger. There were so many people with so many needs—he couldn't do it alone. "Father," he prayed, "please send me the help I need."

Early one evening Jesus arrived on the Bethsaida shore of Galilee, where he saw two fishermen putting their nets into the sea. He called out to them. They pulled in their nets and hurried towards him. They were brothers, Andrew and Simon.

They ate together, and as they talked Jesus realized that God had answered his prayer. "Come with me," Jesus said, "and I will make you fishers of people."

After a brief pause first Simon, then Andrew, stood up and followed Jesus as he walked beside the sea. They met two more fishermen brothers, James and John. Jesus knew that God wanted them to help him too. They were working with their father at the time, but they quickly left him and followed Jesus.

The five of them walked into Capernaum, where Simon and Andrew welcomed everyone into their home. Jesus's friends, being plain, honest fishers, were able to talk to the local people in a way that was easily understood. God had chosen well.

God needed him to speak wherever people gathered, so Jesus visited synagogues and taught from the Bible. One afternoon, a man suddenly came into the place where he was teaching. "What do you want, Jesus of Nazareth?" he shouted. "Have you come to destroy us?"

Jesus heard people around him say that

there must be an evil spirit inside the man. He placed his hand on the man. "Come out of him!" Jesus told the spirit. The poor man fell to the floor, and then was perfectly relaxed.

"Who are you?" somebody asked. "You even have power over evil spirits."

In the early days it was easy for Jesus to find the peace and quiet he needed to pray, to gather his strength, and to think. But news travels faster than human feet, and soon he could no longer enter a village without a crowd coming to him. Sometimes he wanted very much to escape, and his friends tried to protect him, but still the people came.

Jesus saw in their faces that their need for his help was far greater than his need for rest. Some had lost hope, and some were angry. Many were lost. Jesus knew what it was to be human, to feel lost and afraid. How could he turn anybody away? Can any shepherd turn his back on a lost sheep?

The people were poor, but they gave Jesus and his followers food and a place to stay. In one place God sent him Mary Magdalene, a woman who had many problems and wanted very much to be healed. With God's help Jesus was able to heal her, and from then on Mary helped him in his work. She had money of her own, which she gave to the group to do the work of teaching people about God.

Teachers of Jewish law often visited the group at Simon's house, which had become their base.

One afternoon Jesus was talking about forgiveness. "Surely only God can forgive a person who does bad things," one teacher said.

Outside, Jesus could hear the sounds of a crowd gathering. He tried to continue the talk, but after a while it was difficult to continue because of all the noise. Simon jumped to his feet. "They're breaking through my roof!" he cried. It was true.

When the hole was large enough, a sleeping mat, hanging from ropes, was slowly lowered. On the mat was a man. "He is paralyzed," a voice called from the roof. "But we know that you can help him."

Jesus felt their faith move within him as he took the man's hand. "Your sins are forgiven," he said quietly.

Some of the teachers could not believe it. Jesus knew why. Who was Jesus, who was only a man, to forgive people's sins? Saddened because they did not believe and did not seem to want to help, he turned to the paralyzed man. "Pick up your mat and go home," Jesus told the man.

The man was very surprised. He tested his legs. Standing slowly, he got his mat and thanked Jesus. His friends on the roof cheered.

Some of the teachers were unhappy. Having spent their lives studying and obeying the laws given by Moses, it was difficult for them to understand how God's love really worked. Jesus wished they could understand that people must forgive each other, just as God will always find a way to forgive people.

Whenever Jesus healed someone people said it was blasphemy against God. It seemed so hard to show people that God's law is about love and forgiveness. What would it take?

Jesus was worried about something else too.

Jewish law says that the Sabbath must be a special day, when no one can do any work. It's a good law, because it gives people a space in each week to think about what God wants from them, rather than thinking about the day-to-day things in their lives. But many teachers worried too much about the Sabbath's rules, rather than the chance that it gives people to relax and to think.

One Sabbath day, as Jesus entered the synagogue, he saw a man with a sickness in his hand. The room became quiet. People watched, waiting to see whether Jesus would heal him on the Sabbath.

"Stand up," Jesus said to the man. Then he turned to the people. "Which can we do on the Sabbath," he asked them, "good or evil?"

Nobody said a word.

Here was a chance for Jesus to show them both how God helped people and also his power.

Jesus turned back to the man. "Put out your hand."

As the man held out his hand, it began to grow and fill. He moved it around. He opened and closed his fingers. Most people could not believe it, and some did not look happy. Jesus knew then that there were people who would try to stop his work. Most, however, wanted to be shown how to live a good life. They wanted to be pure before God.

The crowds who came to see Jesus continued to grow. Sometimes it was difficult to talk to so many people. He often stood on higher ground to talk so that more could see and hear. When teaching by the lakeside, Jesus used to take a boat onto the water and speak from there.

How could he teach more people? Jesus realized that he needed to choose some special people from among his closest followers, people who could help him spread the message.

Jesus chose twelve. In Simon the fisherman he saw a man who, although he made mistakes — perhaps because of them — could be a rock on which Jesus could build the future. Jesus called him Peter, meaning "rock." He also chose Simon Peter's brother Andrew.

Jesus called James and John "the sons of thunder" because of their powerful preaching.

The others he chose were Philip, Bartholomew, Matthew, Thomas, James bar Alpheus, Thaddeus, another Simon and Judas Iscariot. Jesus asked Judas, an educated man, to take care of the group's money.

Before these men could teach and heal, they still had much to learn. Jesus had to prepare them. "Tell people stories," he advised them.

"If we simply repeat the laws, they'll follow them without understanding. Stories help people to understand how God's law can be used in their own lives. We have to help them to understand God's message in a way that makes sense to them," Jesus said.

Jesus explained how important it was for the twelve to set a good example. "Be generous; don't hide the light of God's love. If you show love and compassion, others will learn from you. Like a seed that grows in good soil, the word of God, if you plant it, will produce a crop a hundred times bigger than what you started with. The seeds will grow without you having to do any more work. This is what God's kingdom is like. We must create the kingdom of God on earth."

There was a difficult problem. Jesus needed to reach as many people as possible, but he did not want a lot of people to notice him. The country was controlled by the Romans, and they did not want trouble, so they usually cooperated with the powerful Jewish people. Jesus didn't want to get into trouble with them.

Though Jesus often asked people not to talk too much about the things he did, people came together in large groups to hear what he had to say, and people needing help continued to try to find him. Having gone across the lake one day, Jesus was greeted on the shore by another crowd, led by Jairus, a synagogue elder. Jairus was very worried.

"My daughter is dying," Jairus wept. "Please help her."

As he followed Jairus through the crowd, Jesus suddenly felt a familiar healing flow of love. He stopped and looked round. "Who touched my robe?" he asked. It must have seemed like a strange question in the middle of a big crowd.

A woman came forward. "I'm so sorry," she said, "it was me. I've been sick for years and no doctor has been able to help me."

"Daughter, your faith has made you better," Jesus said. "Go in peace."

As Jesus got closer to Jairus's house, two men ran out. "Jairus, we're so sorry. She is dead!"

"Don't be afraid," Jesus told Jairus. "Believe."

Jairus took Jesus to where his daughter was. Taking her hand, Jesus spoke to her. "*Talitha koum*. Little lamb, get up."

The child opened her eyes, stood up and walked over to her mother. Jesus asked those within the house to tell nobody what had happened. With such a large crowd waiting outside, however, there was little chance of that.

Jesus hadn't visited his family in Nazareth for almost two years. It was time to return.

His family welcomed him. That Sabbath, in the old synagogue, he read from the scriptures. His former friends and neighbors listened in silence. A cold, angry wind blew towards him from the crowd, making him shiver. It made him think that a storm was coming.

Later, in the street, two men came up to Jesus. "Who do you think you are?" one of them asked. "You're just a worker, Mary's son!" More men gathered.

Jesus was surprised that they seemed to hate him so much. He told myself that a prophet is never welcomed in his own town. Saddened, he walked through the angry crowd. Nobody tried to stop him.

More sad things happened. Jesus got news that the head of John the Baptist had been cut off by King Herod. Herod was weak. Although he had known that John was a good man, he had feared his power. He had let his fear control him. Jesus felt terrible for both John and Herod.

Jesus was living in dangerous times, but God's work had to be done. His twelve friends were now ready for their important work. He sent them off in pairs so they could support each other. "You are now my apostles. God wants you to teach people and to heal," he told them. "Take nothing with you; God will give you everything you need."

Several weeks later the twelve returned, tired but very happy. The group tried to find a quiet place down by the edge of the lake so they could talk about the things that had happened without being disturbed by crowds of people, but it was impossible. The people, like lost sheep looking for their shepherd, followed them. Jesus loved them and could not ignore them. That evening, all five thousand were fed.

At nightfall Jesus told the apostles to take

the boat out on the lake. He would join them later. When he finally found them, there was a big storm. Though their fear sometimes showed that there were weaknesses in their faith, he learned that they had done their work well.

The following morning the group went across Galilee to Gennesaret, where they taught and healed for several days. While they were there, they were watched by some Pharisees, strict teachers of the law. They often came over to talk with the group and challenge Jesus.

One day the group stopped to eat. Hungry and tired, they were enjoying a short rest from the crowds. Jesus saw a group of unhappy looking Pharisees coming near to them. One man, whom Jesus had had trouble with before asked, "Why didn't you do the ritual cleansing before you ate?"

"Nothing can make us impure just by going into our body," Jesus told him.

A lot of people were watching, and a small group gathered round. "This food, coming from the outside, will pass through our stomachs and come out again." Someone laughed. "It is the things that come from the inside—our thoughts and feelings—which have the power to make us clean or unclean," Jesus said.

Jesus was beginning to understand that his work would not be finished until he had given his life, as the scriptures said was going to happen. By sacrificing his own son, God would show that there is nothing that he would not do for people.

Seeking to be closer to God, Jesus took Simon Peter, James and John to the top of a mountain to pray.

More than ever before, Jesus felt that God was near him—it made him remember his baptism in the River Jordan. As he prayed, Jesus was suddenly filled with a deeper understanding. Moses and Elijah appeared beside him and, as at his baptism, he heard God's voice saying, "This is my beloved son."

Later, as he went down from the mountain, Jesus knew what he had to do.

Although his disciples were good men, their faith and understanding sometimes failed them. Jesus knew that his time on earth was limited, so he sometimes felt frustrated by them, the kind of feeling that a loving parent has for their child. "How much longer must I be with you?" Jesus once asked.

And, like children, the disciples sometimes argued amongst themselves about who was the most important. "The one who wants to be the greatest must learn to be the servant of all," Jesus told them.

Once when they were trying to keep Jesus safe from the crowds, the disciples tried to hurry him away from a group of women who had brought their children to be blessed. He stopped them. "Let the children come," he said. "The kingdom of God belongs to people like this."

Innocent, and willing to learn—that is how we should all be before God.

A little later a young man, who was clearly rich, came to Jesus. "Teacher," he asked, "what must I do to enter God's kingdom?"

Jesus smiled. The man really wanted to do what God wanted, but, as was true for so many people, there was something standing between him and God. It was his money. "Sell everything you have and give it to the poor," Jesus told him. "Then follow me."

The man couldn't do it. He turned sadly and walked away. That night Jesus prayed for him.

As Jesus told the disciples, "It is impossible for the rich to enter the kingdom of Heaven. You must give up everything."

"We have given up everything," said Simon Peter.

"And you shall have your reward," Jesus

told him. But he didn't tell Simon Peter how many bad things were going to happen before he got it.

They were getting closer Jerusalem, where it would all end. It was time to prepare his disciples for what was going to happen soon.

"In Jerusalem I will be betrayed to the chief priests," Jesus said. They listened quietly. "They will send me to die. People will laugh at me, hurt me and kill me. Three days later I will rise from the dead." No one said anything, but everyone looked very afraid.

Did this mean Jesus had failed? Many people had heard his message and believed, while others were still trying. However, powerful people were making people's lives even more difficult. Something had to be done to bring a change.

Jesus rode into Jerusalem on a colt, as it said in the scriptures. A crowd followed. More crowds gathered along the way to welcome him. "Hosanna in the highest!" they called, as they tore down palm branches and put them in front of the colt's feet. The palm was a sign of Jewish unity. A threat.

"They welcome you as a king!" said Simon Peter. The disciples were excited. Some of them had been waiting for this. They thought they were finally challenging the right of the Romans to rule over the Jews; even that they were challenging the powerful Jewish leaders. But the real reason for what was going to happen was far greater than any of them could imagine.

"Blessed is he who comes in the name of the Lord!" shouted the crowd.

Jesus's work in Jerusalem had begun. He led the people to the temple to pray, but, because of what he found there, he asked the people to go away and took the disciples out of Jerusalem. He would return the next day.

A temple is supposed to be a peaceful place

where people can hear God's voice. Instead of peace, however, there were people changing money and people selling animals to be killed as gifts for God. Traders were going through the area to save time as they crossed the city, doing business as they went. In what was supposed to be a place of prayer, no one could hear God's voice.

The next morning, at the entrance to the temple, Jesus saw a tough-looking man trying to take tax money from a crying woman. Jesus was so angry that he turned over a table. The disciples started doing the same.

Jesus had to make people see what they were doing. From the top of the steps he called out, "It is written, 'my house will be called a house of prayer for all nations,' but *you* have turned it into a place for thieves!"

The chief priests were angry and afraid. They knew Jesus was right.

The next day Jesus returned to the temple,

where people were now praying happily. A group of priests came up to him. "What authority do you have to do these things?" they asked.

Jesus had God's authority, but he knew that they were looking for a chance to accuse him of blasphemy. He would not answer their question.

Things like this began to happen more often. Jesus could see fear in the faces of his challengers, the fear that would kill him. They tried to trap him using words. How sad they made him feel. Sad and tired.

"Teacher, you are an honest man," began one young man. "Tell us, should we pay taxes to Caesar or not?"

The young man thought that he was going to win. If Jesus answered that they should not pay taxes to Rome, he could be arrested for sedition. If he told them to pay taxes, the weak people would probably stop following him and would not listen to his ideas.

"Why are you trying to trap me?" Jesus asked. "Show me a Roman coin." Jesus held it up. "Whose face is this on the coin?" Everyone knew that it was Caesar's and that the writing on the coin said that he was a god. As this broke one of their commandments, Jews hated the Roman coins.

"Why, it is Caesar," answered the young man.

"Then give to Caesar what is Caesar's, and give to God what is God's. God doesn't need our money, he needs our hearts," Jesus said.

Not all questions were like that. One Pharisee asked Jesus, "Which is the most important of the commandments?"

Jesus could see that he was a good man. "The most important commandment is this," Jesus replied, "that you love God with all your heart, with all your soul, with all your mind, and with all your strength. The second is this: love your neighbor as yourself."

The man smiled. "You are right. To love God and to love each other is more important than anything else."

Jesus smiled. "You are not far from the kingdom of God," he told him.

Though he visited the temple every day, Jesus was staying outside Jerusalem, in the village of Bethany. One evening his group was relaxing after dinner when a woman entered the room, carrying a jar with a long neck that was filled with expensive perfume. Breaking the neck of the jar, she poured some of the perfume over his head.

"What a waste!" exclaimed Judas. "She should have sold the perfume and given the money to the poor."

Poor Judas. After three years of taking care of the group's money, his thinking was natural. "She has done a beautiful thing," Jesus told him. "The poor will always be with you. You can help them any time, but you will not always have me. She poured perfume over me to prepare me for my burial."

Everyone in the room looked unhappy.

It was Passover, the greatest celebration of the Jewish calendar. Some of the disciples went ahead into Jerusalem to find and prepare a room for a meal. Although Jesus had tried to warn them of what was going to happen, they did not realize just how soon the real trouble would begin. This was to be the last meal they would eat together.

After a rather quiet meal, everyone sat at the table. Although the mood was not happy, they were physically and spiritually very close. It was time for Jesus to talk about a difficult issue. These poor men.

"My friends," Jesus began, "very soon one of you will betray me." In fact, the betrayal was already happening, and he knew who it was.

The men could not believe it. The closeness they had been enjoying just seconds before changed into worry and fear. "Surely it is not me!" some exclaimed. "Who is it?"

"It is one who puts bread into the bowl with me."

Judas, who was putting his bread into Jesus's bowl at that moment, quickly pulled back his hand.

Jesus wondered if any of the others had noticed. It was necessary for God's plan that somebody should betray Jesus, but it was a terrible thing to do.

Judas looked very worried. From this moment on, his life would be terrible. In the confusion that followed, Judas stood up weakly from his seat and left the room.

There was still work to be done. Picking up some bread, Jesus thanked God and broke it. Passing it around, he said quietly, "Take this; this is my body." It symbolized all that he was; all that he and the group had shared. Their faces were unhappy. Some cried.

Jesus picked up the wine cup. Again he

thanked God and passed it among the eleven remaining disciples. "This is my blood, God's new promise, poured out for you and for all people."

They understood how important this promise was, but still did not fully understand what Jesus had to do.

That night Jesus went to the Mount of Olives to pray. His friends went with him, but again he had to tell them a painful truth. "Tonight, when they come for me, you will all run away. If you stay with me, you will die." They were only human, after all.

Simon Peter was hurt. "I won't leave you," he said.

He was right. Jesus knew Simon Peter would never leave him, but his courage would have a limit. "Before the morning comes," Jesus told him sadly, "you will disown me three times."

Tonight, more than ever before, Jesus

needed to pray for strength to endure the suffering that was coming. Jesus and the group walked to the garden at Gethsemane, his favorite place on the Mount. Leaving most of the men near the entrance to the garden, Jesus took Peter, James and John with him. "Stay here and keep watch," he told them.

Having walked a short distance away from them, Jesus felt so sad that he fell to the ground. "Father, you can do anything. If it is your will, take this suffering from me." His prayer was not answered. He did not find peace.

Returning to his friends, Jesus found them sleeping. He felt totally alone. "Couldn't you keep watch for just one hour? You must stay awake!" Again he went to pray, but when he returned they had gone to sleep again. Jesus felt terrible. His prayers had still not been answered.

On his third try Jesus finally found God's calming presence. He gave Jesus courage and made him feel better, and told him again that this was the work for which he had been born. Jesus found his friends were sleeping again. He woke them. When Jesus looked up, he saw Judas coming with a group of armed men.

"Here comes my betrayer," Jesus said quietly.

Smiling, but ashamed to meet Jesus's eye, Judas greeted him and identified him with a kiss. Jesus wanted to make Judas feel better, but there was no time. The guards grabbed Jesus. He tried to explain to them what they were doing, but they wouldn't listen.

As they led Jesus away he accepted that the scriptures must be fulfilled. His disciples were gone.

The chief priest called his council together. There was never any doubt about what would happen at Jesus's trial. He felt very bad for those who told lies about him. Then the chief priest asked him, "Are you the Son of God?"

"I am," Jesus replied. "You will see me sitting at God's right hand."

"You heard that!" the priest shouted. He tore his clothes, a sign that Jesus must die.

Jesus saw Simon Peter hiding nearby, watching. His poor friend. What fear, what pain he must be feeling. The morning came, but Jesus knew Simon Peter would never leave him. When he was no longer there, he would be Jesus's rock, his foundation.

Early next morning they took Jesus to Pontius Pilate, the Roman governor of the province. He questioned Jesus, asking, "Are you the King of the Jews?"

Jesus knew Pontius Pilate wanted him to say that he wasn't so he could let him go, but Jesus couldn't help him.

There was a big crowd outside. Jesus was used to crowds, but this one was different. Although he knew some people in the sea of faces, many more were strangers who had come to see what would happen to him.

Priests were among the people, whispering, preparing them for their roles in what was to come.

Pilate saw only one way to avoid responsibility. He handed the decision to the crowd so that he would not have to make it. "What shall I do with the King of the Jews?" he asked.

At first just a few voices called, "Crucify him!" but it soon grew into a loud, steady chant. "Crucify him! Crucify him!"

"Why? What was his crime?" asked Pilate.

The crowd wanted blood.

Jesus was to be crucified. It was going to be terrible. The whips would remove his flesh from his bones. People had died from this alone. Later, they would put spikes through his arms, nailing him to a piece of wood. They would attach it to another piece of wood and put another spike into his ankles. When his arms and legs could no longer support his weight, he would not be able to breathe, and he would die.

God would feel human suffering through him — his own son — to show that his love and forgiveness have no limits. Though Jesus was weak and tired, he had to carry the wood for his own cross to a nearby cliff called Golgotha, "the place of the skull."

When Jesus could not carry it well, soldiers pulled a man from the crowd to help him. At Golgotha, other soldiers drove in the spikes. The pain made it hard to breathe and hard to think, but he found the words to forgive. Then he prayed, trusting that people would finally understand and could start again. It was only his body that they hurt.

Jesus's final hours were long. As the end got near, he remembered a song to God from the scriptures, a song of sadness and hope:

My God, why have you forsaken me? You are the holy one. Our fathers trusted you and were saved, but I am hated by everyone. All who see me make fun of me, saying, "He trusted in the Lord; let the Lord rescue him."

Since before I was born you have been my God.

Do not be far from me, for trouble is near and there is no one to help.

I am poured out like water and all my bones are out of joint, my heart is like melted wax.

My throat is dry and my tongue sticks to the roof of my mouth.

You put me in the dust of death.

People stare and gloat over me.

They divide my clothes among them.

Lord, do not be far from me.

Then Jesus's human suffering ended, but he would come back from death in three days.

He still had to explain to his friends that his death had opened up a new way to God for everyone. Only when they understood this would he be free to go up to his father in heaven.

Siddhartha Gautama:
The Life of the Buddha

R.N. Pillai

【主な登場人物、地名など】

Suddhodana シュッドーダナ《シャーキヤ族の王、釈迦の実父》

Sakya シャーキヤ《地名、部族名》

Mahamaya マーヤー夫人《釈迦の生母》

Asita アシタ仙人

Kondanna コンダンニャ《占師》

Prajapati Gotami プラジャーパティー・ゴータミー《釈迦の叔母で養母》

Devadatta デーヴァダッタ《釈迦のいとこ》

Yashodhara ヤショーダラー《釈迦の正妃》

Channa チャンナ《馬丁》

Kapilavastu カピラヴァストゥ《シャーキヤ族の都》

Kanthaka カンタカ《白馬の名》

Magadha マガダ国

Rajagriha ラージャグリハ《マガダ国の首都》

Bimbisara ビンビサーラ《マガダ国の王》

Alara Kalama アーラーラ・カーラーマ《思想家》

Uddaka Ramputta ウッダカ・ラーマプッタ《思想家》

Sujata スジャータ《釈迦に乳がゆを供養した娘》

Gaya ガヤー、ブッダガヤ《地名》

Mara マーラ《悪魔、魔神》

Anathapindika アナータピンディカ《コーサラ国の長者》

Kosala コーサラ国

Jeta monastery 祇園精舎《寺院》

Ajatasatru アジャータシャトル《マガダ国の王》

Angulimala アングリマーラ《弟子の一人》

Kisa Gautami キサー・ゴータミー《子どもを亡くした女性》

Chunda チュンダ《釈迦の最期の布施者》

sukaramaddava スーカラ・マッダヴァ《キノコを使った料理》

Kusinara クシナラ《村の名》

Subhadda スバッダ《弟子の一人》

Two thousand six hundred years ago a wise and good king, Suddhodana, lived in a place called Sakya in the Himalaya mountains of northern India. One of Suddhodana's wives was Mahamaya.

One full moon night, as Queen Mahamaya was sleeping, she had a beautiful dream. She felt she was being carried away by *devas* from heaven to a sacred lake in the Himalayas. There she was given a bath and dressed in beautiful clothes. A white elephant carrying a silver lotus flower walked around her three times before entering her womb.

When the king heard about the dream, he invited sixty-four brahmin astrologers to tell him what the meaning was. They told him, "you will have a son who will give up the kingdom so that he can get great wisdom. He will save all the world's people."

When it was time for her baby to be born, Queen Mahamaya went to have it in the home where she had been born. King Suddhodana made plans for her to be taken to the house of the Koliyas, her own family. As they reached a beautiful place called the Lumbini Garden, the queen knew the baby would come out soon. The curtains were closed around her. She stood under a *sala* tree holding one of its branches, and her son was born. But there was no pain at all. The baby's body glowed bright. He stood up and took seven steps. At each step, a lotus flower grew quickly under his feet.

"I am the chief of all worlds," said the baby. "I have no equal. I am supreme. This is the last time I will be born into the world." It was full moon day in the late spring month of Vaisakha, which was May of the year 566 BCE.

Everyone in the king's family was very excited that his son had been born.

News traveled quickly that a very special child had been born to King Suddhodana and Queen Mahamaya. Asita, a wise man, came to see the child. He picked up the child in his arms and started to cry.

A worried Suddhodana asked Asita, "Is anything wrong with the baby?"

"No," said Asita. "Your baby will be an all-enlightened Buddha who will teach all humans the greatest truth. Sadly I won't be able to hear him because I will no longer be alive then. I am sorry for myself. That is why I cry."

When it was time to give the baby a name, King Suddhodana invited eight brahmin astrologers. Seven of them said that the child had two possible futures. "If he chooses power," they told the king, "he will be a sceptre-wielding *loka chakravarti*, an emperor of the world. But if he takes the spiritual path, he will be a *dharmic chakaravarti*, a spiritual emperor, teaching everyone the truth about life. And how will his future be decided? If he sees four unhappy things—an old man, a sick man, a dead body, and a monk—he is sure to turn away from the worldly life."

The eighth astrologer, Kondanna, an eighteen-year-old brahmin, said, "This baby will be none other than a Buddha."

The astrologers named the child Siddhartha, meaning "he who has found meaning."

Sadly, Queen Mahamaya died just seven days after Siddhartha was born. Prajapati Gotami, another of Suddhodana's wives, began to take care of Siddhartha. She gave her own son Nanda to a nurse to take care of.

Each year King Suddhodana used a golden plow in a field. As this took place soon after Siddhartha's birth, he left the baby in the care of nurses, and stepped into the field and took his place behind the plow. The nurses wanted to see everything, so they left the child at the foot of a rose apple tree and went to watch.

When they returned, they saw something amazing—the child was sitting in the lotus position, or *padmasana*, in meditation. The shadow of the rose apple tree, rather than moving as the sun moved, had stayed in the same place all the time, protecting him from the hot sun. On hearing this the king bowed to the child.

As Siddhartha grew up he was both a great student and a warrior. The young prince was charming and kind, and he was given anything that he wanted.

King Suddhodana was careful that his son did not have any chances to hear about or feel unhappy things of any kind. Three beautiful homes were built for Siddhartha to live in, one for each season, with high walls that kept him from seeing the outside world.

Prince Siddhartha Gautama cared about all living beings. One day while he was walking in the forest, his cousin Devadatta took his bow and arrow and shot down a bird that was flying above them. Both of them ran towards the fallen bird; Siddhartha reached it first and took hold of the bird, which was fighting for its life. He pulled out the arrow, put healing herbs on the place where it hit the bird, and touched the bird softly.

"Give the bird to me," Devadatta said. "I shot it down."

Siddhartha said no. "Had you killed the bird," he told his cousin, "it would have been yours. I have saved its life, so it is mine. Let us go to the court of wise men and ask them to decide."

The court of wise men said that a life belongs to one who saves it, not to one who tries to destroy it.

Although he had all of the best things in life and was protected from the bad things that happened in the world, Siddhartha always seemed like he was thinking about something.

This worried King Suddhodana, who was always worried that the astrologers' prediction might come true. "What will happen if my son chooses to leave everything behind and take the spiritual road? There will be no one to become king after I am gone."

The king did everything he could to make Siddhartha think about other things. Siddhartha's home was filled with music and dance. The king told everyone that they could not talk about anything that was not happy when the young prince was there. But Siddhartha still seemed to be thinking about something important.

"He should be married," the wise men said to Suddhodana. All the beautiful young women from the area were invited in the hope that Siddhartha would choose one of them to be his wife. The prince gave presents to all those who came, but specially favored a girl called Yashodhara. She belonged to the Koliya clan, and was Suddhodana's niece and Devadatta's sister.

The royal wedding between Siddhartha and Yashodhara was celebrated all over the country. Now Suddhodana felt better—the young couple looked like they were very much in love. But Prince Siddhartha was still thinking about something.

"The high walls will keep my son from the outside world," Suddhodana kept telling himself.

One day Siddhartha asked Suddhodana, "Father, may I go out and take a look at how the other people live?"

"Yes my son," his father said. "You may, but I have to get things ready first."

The king had flags and beautiful things put up all along the roads, and was careful that his son would not see anything sad.

The prince went with Channa, a chariot driver. Suddenly they saw an old man with no teeth and silver hair. He was dressed in old, dirty clothes. He needed a stick to walk.

Siddhartha saw the old man, but did not understand what he was seeing.

"What is that, Channa?" he asked.

"It is old age, which will happen to everyone someday," Channa explained.

The prince was unhappy with what he had seen and told Channa to drive home. Siddhartha now knew that one day he, too, would grow old, and would have grey hair and no teeth.

"Is there no escape from old age?" the prince asked himself.

The prince wanted to see more, so he asked his father to let him go to the city of Kapilavastu. Suddhodana did not want Siddhartha to go, but he agreed. Dressed as a normal man and again traveling with Channa, he walked the city streets, where he saw many kinds of workers.

Suddenly, as if from nowhere, Siddhartha saw a man lying on the ground in pain. He was holding his stomach and crying out loudly. There were purple spots all over his body, and he could not breathe well.

The kind prince sat beside the man and put the man's head on his lap.

"Channa, tell me, what is the matter with this man?"

"O prince," said Channa, "he is sick. His body is burning all over. Please do not touch him, as you may also become sick."

Siddhartha realized that there must be many people who, like this man, had painful sicknesses. He returned to the palace with a sad heart.

Siddhartha now wanted to find out more about life in the outside world. He dressed as a young man from a rich family and again went out to see the city with Channa. He saw four men carrying a body, which was lying quite still. Crying men and women followed the body, which was put down on some wood.

Both wood and body were then set on fire.

"What is this, Channa?" asked the prince. "Why does that man let himself be burned?"

"He is dead, Prince Siddhartha."

"Will everyone die? Is this what death looks like?"

"Every living being has to die," said Channa. "There is no escape for anyone."

Siddhartha went back to the palace. He found it hard to understand that death could not be stopped. "Surely there must be a way to put an end to death," he thought to himself. "I must find out how."

When the prince went to the city for the fourth time, he saw a monk with a peaceful-looking face. The monk was dressed in orange.

"Who is he, Channa?" asked Siddhartha.

"He is a monk," answered Channa. "He lives in a temple and supports himself with alms, teaching people how to live a good and religious life."

"Yes, I will be a monk like him," Siddhartha said to himself as he returned home.

Sitting in the garden later that day, Siddhartha received news that his wife had had a baby boy, their first child. The boy was named Rahula, meaning obligation.

Siddhartha was worried that even if people tried hard to live happy lives, all their efforts led only to dying. He felt very afraid of the idea of death. "Is there no way out?" he asked himself. "Does everything have to end? There must be another way." He was starting to think that he should spend his life trying to find an alternative to death, to search for a way to live forever—if that was possible.

It was now time for him to leave behind the happy life of the palace. Siddhartha asked Channa to get his favorite horse, Kanthaka, ready. In the middle of the night, as he was about to leave, he stopped to take one last look at his wife and newborn son. He stood and looked at the sleeping mother and child. He wanted to kiss his son, but he was afraid that it would wake his wife up.

"However hard it is to leave," Siddhartha said to himself, "love for one's wife and child is nothing compared with love for all the people in the world."

Siddhartha went off into the darkness, together with Channa. When they got to the River Anoma at the border with the nearby kingdom of Magadha, the prince got off his horse, took off all his jewelry and beautiful clothes, and handed them to Channa.

"Take these and ride back to my father on Kanthaka," he told Channa. "Tell him that I am going to find out if there is a way to overcome old age, sickness and death. If I find it, I'll return and teach you all."

As he turned to walk on alone, Kanthaka did not move. "Kanthaka, go with Channa. Do not wait for me," said Siddhartha. Kanthaka began to cry. It fell down dead because it was so sad that it could not go with Siddhartha.

After Channa had left, Siddhartha cut off all his hair, changed into monk's clothing, and began walking.

After a while, Siddhartha came to the city of Rajagriha, where Bimbisara, the wise king of Magadha, lived. Reports reached Bimbisara that a very good-looking young man was traveling around his kingdom.

Bimbisara, a very spiritual man, went to meet him. He thought Siddhartha was so wonderful that he offered his daughter and half his kingdom to him. But Siddhartha did not want either of them. "I am trying to find a way to end all human suffering," he told the king. "I cannot stay. I will return when I have found the answer."

Hearing about what Siddhartha was trying to do, five of his friends also left home and traveled to join him. One of them was Kondanna, who had said that Siddhartha would be none other than a Buddha.

Siddhartha and the others all became students of a great teacher called Alara Kalama. He taught them a kind of meditation called *samatha* to calm the mind and free it from inner turmoil. Siddhartha was very good at it, and quickly rose to the seventh level.

"This good feeling that you experience in the seventh stage will be with you even after death," Alara Kalama told his students.

"But have you nothing more to teach?" Siddhartha asked the teacher. "There are still so many things which we do not know. I must have an answer to old age, sickness and death."

"I have taught you all I know," said Alara Kalama. "You now know as much as me. If you are not satisfied, you must go to Uddaka, the son of Rama, who will teach you the eighth and last stage of *samatha* meditation."

Siddhartha and his friends left Alara

Kalama and walked through the woods of Magadha until they found Uddaka Ramputta. With his help Siddhartha moved up to the eighth stage of *samatha* meditation. Uddaka could not believe it.

"You are now my equal," he said. "You must stay here as a teacher."

"But old age, sickness and death—how can they be stopped?" asked Siddhartha.

"I do not have an answer to that," said Uddaka. "I am only a teacher after all. But the level of *samatha* meditation that you have now achieved will stay with you even after you die."

Siddhartha and his five friends said goodbye to Uddaka and went away.

At that time in India many people believed that one way of finding out the ultimate truth was to test the body. They tried to eat as little food as possible. Siddhartha and his friends wanted to try it. They ate very little, and they meditated in the open air, even when the weather was bad.

Siddhartha began eating less and less. At first, he ate only roots of plants, leaves and fruit. Finally, he ate only cow dung. He became so thin that his legs and arms looked like sticks of bamboo. When he meditated, he held his breath for so long that he felt terrible pain. Wearing only rags, he meditated in the hot summer sun and the cold of winter.

For six long years he continued in this way, but still did not find any answers. One day he fainted, and would have died if a shepherd had not given him a little milk. Having been so close to death and still without any new understanding, he decided that giving up food until he died was not the answer—he needed to eat enough to stay alive.

When his five friends saw that Siddhartha had started eating again, they left him in disgust. But Siddhartha had learned something very important—that there was a different way to live. You did not need to give up worldly comforts, but you did not need to be self-indulgent either. It was possible to choose a middle path, or *madhyama marga*.

In the nearby village of Senani lived a beautiful and rich girl named Sujata. One morning she was getting ready to give an offering to the tree god. She sent her maid to clean the area under the banyan tree near the River Neranjara.

When the maid came back, she was very excited. She told Sujata, "The tree god has come in person to receive your offering. He is sitting under the tree meditating."

Sujata was now excited too, and they were filled with joy when they saw a young figure sitting under the tree. They thought he must be a god come in answer to their prayers. It was of course Siddhartha, who took the offering of sweet milk porridge before crossing the river on his way towards Gaya.

When he reached Gaya, Siddhartha looked for a good place to meditate. He sat under a large banyan tree. With his face turned towards the east, he began meditating. He promised himself that he would not stop until he had discovered the highest wisdom. Here he practiced a way of meditating called *anapana sati* or "awareness of breathing," concentrating as fully as possible on each breath.

While Siddhartha was meditating, a spirit called Mara came to seduce him by showing him the things he had chosen to give up. Mara came to Siddhartha with a large army and started to attack him, but the arrows turned into flowers and fell at Siddhartha's feet. Mara then tried to tempt Siddhartha with his three beautiful daughters, but Siddhartha continued meditating.

It was again full moon night in the month of Vaisakha, the month in which Siddhartha had been born. He was now thirty-five years old. As he meditated on this special night, something happened to Siddhartha's mind. He began seeing his past lives. He had been born as a god many times. He had been kings. He had been born millions of times.

He continued to meditate, and as the night went on he began to understand the truth about life and death. He understood that things never really end and start but come around again and again. All the things a person does in their life, both the good things and the bad things, have an effect on what will happen in their next life. Everything has a reason, everything has a result—this is the circle of *karma*.

The night was ending, and Siddhartha understood how everything in the world is connected with everything else. Nothing exists by itself. Nothing can be ignored; nothing can be left out; everything is important.

By the time morning came Siddhartha had become the Buddha, which means "the enlightened one." He knew the truth of everything. He had the answer for the riddle of life, had discovered the cause of sadness, and found the answer to old age, sickness and death. From this time on he would become known as the Lord Buddha, and the banyan tree where he found enlightenment, or *bodhi*, became known as the Bodhi Tree.

The Lord Buddha remained under the Bodhi Tree in Gaya for another seven weeks, enjoying the feeling of his new freedom. In the fourth week he created a beautiful jeweled chamber to meditate in.

One day it started raining, and a huge king cobra appeared from the forest. It made itself into a round cushion for the Buddha to sit on. The snake sheltered the Buddha's head from the rain with its hood. When the rain stopped, the cobra turned into a beautiful young man who paid his respects to the Buddha. He was a god who had come from heaven.

On the fiftieth morning, two merchants called Tapussa and Bhallika came. They gave the Buddha rice cakes and honey. The Buddha pulled a few pieces of hair from his head and gave it to them as a gift. These pieces of hair, called *kesadhatu*, are kept even now in the famous Shwedagon Pagoda.

Towards the end of Buddha's time under the Bodhi Tree, the high god Brahma Sahampati came and asked the Buddha to teach the things that he had learned, the principles, or *dharma*, that gave order to the universe, so that everyone could benefit from them.

The Buddha decided that he would start by teaching the five friends who had studied with him. They now lived in the city of Kasi, so Buddha went to find them there.

"Look," they said when they saw him, "Siddhartha is coming, that lover of luxury. Don't listen to anything he says." But as the Buddha came closer they could easily see that this was not the same old Siddhartha, but a divine being. The monks took his bowl and robe and put them down gently; they prepared a seat for him, and one of them hurried off to get water to wash the Buddha's feet.

The Buddha took his seat, and began to tell them what he now understood. "I have found the way to that peaceful state of mind called *nirvana*, beyond all pain and death. In *nirvana*, you can know a happiness that no one else can understand."

The five monks were not sure if they should believe him. "Siddhartha, how did you enter *nirvana* from living a soft life, when you could not do it by living a hard one?"

"I am no longer your friend, and I am no longer a human or a god. You now see before you the Buddha, the *tathagata*, the one beyond all earthly comings and goings. And believe me," he said, "I have not lived an easy life. By taking the middle path, avoiding self-indulgence on the one hand and self-mortification on the other, I have arrived at *nirvana*. If you follow my teachings, you, too, will find it."

The Buddha then explained to the monks the four noble truths that are at the center of Buddhism.

The first noble truth is that everyone must feel suffering and pain at some point in their lives, including sickness, aging and death. But because we all feel pain, it is something to learn from.

The second noble truth is that sadness and spiritual pain come from wanting things, again feelings shared by everyone which we can all learn from.

The third noble truth is that pain and sadness can be overcome by understanding what they mean.

The fourth noble truth is that sadness and spiritual pain do not last. There are things we can do in our lives to overcome them.

The five monks listened carefully to what Lord Buddha told them. "So what must we do to overcome sadness?" one of them asked.

The Buddha then told them what he had learned about the middle way and told his friends about "the eightfold path" to eliminate suffering. He told them about the eight ways to understand how the world works, and said that they should meditate on each one so they could understand for themselves what each of them meant.

Each part of the eightfold path starts with the word "right," which Lord Buddha explained means "perfect," something to work towards.

The first of the eight is right perspective, learning to see the world as it really is rather than how we or other people would like it to be. The second is right intention, or doing things for good reasons.

The third is right speech, or choosing carefully what we say. The fourth is right conduct, not acting in ways that are harmful to ourselves or to others.

The fifth is right livelihood, not having harmful jobs, while the sixth is right endeavor, doing things in a careful, thoughtful way.

The seventh is right attention, keeping our minds on whatever it is we are doing, and the eighth is right concentration, giving everything necessary to what we are doing at the time.

Finally, Lord Buddha showed the monks how he had learned to meditate, thinking about his breathing to keep himself focused. He called this way of meditating *vipassana*.

By the time Lord Buddha had finished explaining the Buddhist way to the five monks, they knew that this was true enlightenment and became Lord Buddha's first students.

The Buddha now started to travel all over, and many people joined the Buddhist community, or *sangha*. Siddhartha's father, King Suddhodana, heard of the Buddha's teachings, and asked his son to pay a visit to him at Kapilavastu, the home that he left.

Yashodhara set eyes on the husband who had left her seven years ago. She realized that this was no longer Prince Siddhartha, but the Buddha, who had found the truth. She turned to her and Siddhartha's son. "Rahula, this is your father," she said. The Buddha had no material wealth to give but let Rahula join the *sangha* as a monk.

At that time India used the caste system. People were divided into higher and lower social groups. The Buddha did not believe in it, and men and women from all levels of society joined him. Upali, the great Buddhist monk, was originally a barber; another disciple, Sunita, came from a poor family which took dead flowers from shrines.

Buddha's attendant was his cousin Ananda.

The Buddha's two most important disciples, Sariputta and Mahamoggallana, and came from rich families. While the pure Sariputta had been a good person since he was a boy, Mahamoggallana—who had magical powers and was said to be able to speak with the dead and fly through the air—had done bad things.

While he was traveling in Magadha, Mahamoggallana was killed by robbers. When asked why Mahamoggallana had not fought back and saved himself, Buddha explained that Mahamoggallana had killed his parents in another life, so there was nothing that he could do to stop his death in this life.

Anathapindika, was a rich man from Kosala. He followed the Buddha, and he became famous for helping the Buddhist *sangha*. He gave these monks food and a place to stay; sometimes there were as many as a hundred monks staying in his house.

Even this was not enough for Anathapindika. He decided that he would buy the garden of Prince Jeta and make it into a monastery.

"What is the price of your garden?" he asked the prince.

"The price? Fill the entire garden with gold, that is the price," said Jeta, never expecting Anathapindika to take him seriously.

Jeta was very surprised when he saw Anathapindika bringing enough gold coins to cover the ground. He was so impressed that the prince gave the garden to the *sangha* for free.

The Lord Buddha wanted to do something to say thank you to Anathapindika. The night before he died, Anathapindika visited Buddha at the Jeta monastery, as he did several times each day. Lord Buddha blessed him and told him he would be remembered as long as any god.

Not everyone understood Lord Buddha's teachings. There was a man named Devadatta, who was the Buddha's own cousin and brother-in-law. Devadatta had joined the *sangha* and learned a little, but greed and feelings of hate entered his mind.

King Bimbisara of Magadha had been one of the first people who helped Siddhartha, but his son Ajatasatru was jealous. Devadatta and Ajatasatru told King Bimbisara to abdicate. Ajatasatru became the king, put his father in prison and killed him.

Devadatta's evil plans did not stop there. He told Ajatasatru to make Nalagiri, the royal elephant, attack the Buddha. Nalagiri ran towards Buddha, but fell at his feet, subdued by his goodness. Next Devadatta sent men to kill the Buddha, but when they heard his teachings, they became his students. Finally, Devadatta pushed a very large stone down at the Buddha. However, it did nothing more than scratch the great teacher's toe.

In the end Devadatta understood that the things he had done were wrong, and he traveled to where the Buddha was to say that he was sorry. As he arrived at the monastery, the earth opened up and swallowed him.

Another famous story is about robber who came to be known as Angulimala or "garland of fingers." He was the son of the chaplain to the king of Kosala—he was clever and often got into trouble. When he was born his father named him Ahimsaka, meaning "the harmless one," but that didn't save him.

He was sent to study under a well-known teacher, but the other students were jealous because Ahimsaka learned so quickly. They tried to make his teacher dislike him.

The teacher told Ahimsaka that his studies were now finished, but as a final gift, the teacher said he must bring him a thousand fingers, each taken from a different person. He thought that his student would be killed by someone as he tried to get the fingers.

Ahimsaka moved into the jungle, where

he would attack people, kill them and cut off their fingers. He then put the fingers together into a garland, or *mala*, which he wore round his neck. This was when everyone started calling him Angulimala.

Finally Angulimala needed just one more finger to complete his garland for the teacher, but by this time the king's army was close to finding him. Fearing for her son's life, Angulimala's mother ran into the jungle one night to warn him of the danger. "Here comes my last victim," Angulimala thought.

Angulimala was about to attack her. But Lord Buddha saw what was about to happen, and he appeared in place of Angulimala's mother. All night long Angulimala followed the Buddha, axe in hand, but whenever he was almost close enough to attack, the Buddha would disappear and then appear again in another place. When it was almost morning Angulimala shouted, "Stop!"

Without turning, Lord Buddha said, "I

have stopped, but you haven't. I have stopped killing living things, but you haven't learned that." At that moment the Buddha turned to look at Angulimala, and the robber fell to the ground, his sword flying from his hand.

The next morning, when the king visited the Buddha, he was surprised to see Angulimala in a monk's yellow robes. As the Angulimala had already become a monk, the king did not have him killed.

When Angulimala went around asking for money or food, people who had lost their family members because of him threw stones at him, and he would return home bleeding and hurt. The Buddha said, "It is better to receive punishment here and now than to go to hell, which is where you would have gone because of the bad things that you did."

The Buddha and his students never forgot that the search for the middle way had started with the important question of why we all have to suffer and die, and it was not surprising that these were the things which he talked about again and again in his teachings.

To anyone who asked him, Buddha would say that we must all be born, get older and die. This is a natural thing that teaches us that we should value and feel thankful for our life.

Death, he told everyone, is not the end of life. It is just the end of the body we are in during this life. Life is like water in a river—just because the water has passed by does not mean the river does not exist anymore.

Buddha explained how the fear of death come from the fear of losing our identity and place in the world. We know that we will die long before we do—this helps us to understand that everything is changing all the time, and how important it is to value what we have right now.

One day a woman called Kisa Gautami came to the Buddha carrying her dead child.

She was very sad, and asked the Buddha, "Please use your powers to bring my child back to life."

The Buddha said, "Bring me some mustard seeds from a house where no one has ever died."

Kisa Gautami went from door to door all around the area, asking for mustard seeds, but she could not find even one house where no one had ever died. Kisa Gautami now understood what the great teacher was saying, and returned to the Buddha thinking about how everyone in the world must die. She joined the women's monastery, and when she died, she entered *nirvana*.

Another important thing that Buddha was always being asked by his followers was about *karma*, the understanding that everything a person does in their life has an effect on what will happen in their next life.

"Do we have any control over what

becomes our own *karma*?" asked one person.

"Yes, you do," said Buddha. "Think of *karma* as something you choose to do, not something that happens to you. *Karma* can only come from an action that you think about doing; if there is no will, there can be no *karma*."

"So what sort of actions are involved in creating *karma*?" asked the person.

"*Karma* can be created by body, mind and things you say," explained Buddha. "Hurting another living thing, stealing, lying, speaking mean words and anger will all bring you bad *karma*. Kindness, thinking about others, generosity, thoughtfulness—all will bring you good *karma*."

It was sometimes hard for Buddha's followers to understand his ideas, so he often explained them using simple stories.

To teach about the importance of right intention, he told a story about a beggar woman who bought a small oil lamp and placed it in front of Buddha's monastery. The tiny lamp looked so ridiculous that a monk wanted to put it out. He tried his best to put out the flame, but he could not. Buddha walked by and said to the monk, "The intention behind the action of leaving that lamp was so pure and so strong that you would not be able to put the flame out even with all the waters of the four oceans."

In another example of right intention, Buddha told the story of Velama, a brahmin, who had given away hundreds of gifts — bowls of gold and silver filled with jewels, expensive cushions and fine pieces of cloth. When he died, he found that he had not been gone to highest heaven, and could not understand why. "The reason," said the Buddha, "is that Velama had given his gifts to people who did not deserve them. Had Velama given just one or two of his gifts to someone who was worthy of them then he would have gone to the highest heaven."

To explain right endeavor and right conduct the Buddha told of some little boys who were playing on a road when Buddha passed by with his alms bowl. Seeing the Lord, one of the boys found some sand and put it into the bowl, as he did so imagining that he was giving the Buddha gold. Because of this simple but heartfelt gift, the boy was later born again as a prince.

The Buddha was now nearing the age of 80 and was growing weak. He told Ananda, his attendant, that he had decided that he would leave the world in less than three months.

Together with Ananda, Buddha started traveling, teaching people about *dharma* in all the places he visited. At last he arrived at a place called Pava. One of Buddha's rich students, Chunda, invited the Buddha and monks to join him for lunch. The meal included a food called *sukaramaddava*, made with truffles.

Buddha spoke quietly to Chunda, saying, "Chunda, I would like you to give the *sukaramaddava* only to me."

"So be it," said Chunda. He gave the food to the Buddha, but not to any of the other monks.

Buddha called Chunda again. "Chunda, I would like you to put all the *sukaramaddava* that is left in a deep hole in the ground. It should be eaten only by a master, and not by any other living being." Again Chunda did as he had been asked.

Lord Buddha had chosen that his death be brought about by eating the *sukaramaddava*, which he knew had poison in it, and he knew that he had only a few days left in his body. They continued traveling until they arrived in the jungle country of Kusinara, where they rested by some *sala* trees. This is where Buddha would meet his last disciple.

Hearing that the Buddha was nearby, a monk named Subhadda came quickly in the hope of meeting the master. Ananda stopped him. "The Buddha is tired," he told Subhadda. "Do not talk to him now."

The Buddha heard what they were saying. "Let him in, Ananda," he said. "He is someone who wants to know the truth."

Subhadda, who had studied under many famous teachers of the time, asked the Buddha, "What do you think of all these teachers? Are their teachings right?"

"Do not worry about whether they are right or wrong," said Buddha. "I shall teach you the true way." And so the Buddha then taught his last lesson to his very last student.

"What is important is the eightfold path. It is the only way for a person to become a true saint. If a teacher teaches that path, then true enlightenment will follow; if the path is absent, so too will enlightenment be absent."

Subhadda then left, and the Buddha turned to Ananda. "It may be, Ananda," he said, "that people will say that without the Buddha, the great teacher, there will be no teacher. You should not think in this way. It is the lessons that I have taught which should be your teacher when I am gone."

Lord Buddha's time was nearly at an end, and he spoke to his monks, the *bhikkus*, one last time. "If any of you still have any doubts about the Buddha and the teaching, you should ask me now so that you will not feel bad that you did not ask me while I was still with you."

None of the monks said anything. None had any questions. All stayed quiet.

The Buddha said, "Perhaps it is because I am your teacher that you do not question me." But the monks stayed quiet.

Next Ananda got to his feet. "My Lord," he said to Buddha, "I believe that in this group of monks there is not one who has a single doubt or question about the Buddha and his teachings."

Then the Buddha looked one last time

around the *bhikkus*. "O monks," he said, "these are my very last words to you. *Vaya dhamma sankhara, appamadena sampadetha.* Every single thing in the world can change. Nothing lasts forever. Each of you must work hard for your own salvation."

These were the Buddha's very last words.

He lay back on the couch among the *sala* trees in the lion posture, on his right side with both legs stretched, his left hand resting on his left thigh and his right hand supporting his head.

Word had already spread that Buddha was about to leave the world, and many, many people started coming into the area. The word of his passing reached heaven, and the gods came together in the sky above.

The Buddha then lay still, closed his eyes, and traveled through all the levels of consciousness. It was a spiritual journey that the Buddha alone could make, into the ultimate reality.

Muhammad:
The Life of the Prophet

Ahmed Abo Knegar

【主な登場人物、地名など】

Abd al-Muttalib アブド・アル・ムッタリブ《ムハンマドの父方の祖父》

Kaaba カアバ神殿《最高の聖地とみなされている聖殿》

Abdullah アブドゥッラーフ《ムハンマドの父》

Amina アーミナ《ムハンマドの母》

Bedouin ベドウィン（族）《アラブ系の遊牧民》

Halima ハリーマ《ムハンマドの養母》

Quraysh クライシュ族《マッカ（メッカ）の支配権を握っていた商業貴族》

Yathrib ヤスリブ《町の名。のちのマディーナ》

Abu Talib アブー＝ターリブ《ムハンマドの叔父》

Bahira バヒラ《キリスト教の修道士》

al-Amin アル・アミン《ムハンマドの通り名》

Khadija ハディージャ《ムハンマドの最初の妻》

Qur'an クルアーン（コーラン）《イスラム教の聖典》

al-Aqsa mosque アル＝アクサー・モスク

mountain of Thawr サウル山

Hijra ヒジュラ、聖遷

Medina マディーナ（メディナ）《地名》

Aisha アーイシャ《ムハンマドの3番目の妻》

Badr バドル《地名》

Uhud ウフド山

Qurayzah クライザ族《ユダヤ教徒の部族》

Aws アウス族《アラブ人の部族》

Hudaybiyya フダイビーヤ《マッカ郊外の小村》

Bakr バクル族《マッカと同盟する遊牧民》

Khuza'a クザア族《アラブ人の部族》

hajj ハッジ《マッカへの巡礼》

Mount Arafat アラファト山

Abd al-Muttalib walked to the shrine of the Kaaba in the city of Mecca. Old Abd al-Muttalib was worried, thinking about his son Abdullah, who had died seven months earlier, only two months after marrying Amina. Yet Abdullah had given Amina a wonderful gift, a baby that was going to be born that night.

Abd al-Muttalib reached the Kaaba, where he asked God to give him a fine grandson to make up for the loss of his son. As the sun rose, he heard a sound behind him. He looked up to see Amina's maid rushing towards him.

"My lady has just had a baby boy!" she told him.

When he reached Amina's house, Abd al-Muttalib told Amina how happy he was about her baby and gave him a kiss.

"What name should he be given?" asked Amina.

Abd al-Muttalib gave no answer, but stood up with the baby in his arms. He went quickly to the Kaaba and walked around it, thanking God for the wonderful gift. There were many possible names, but suddenly he heard the child's name in his heart: Muhammad. This would be the baby's name. The name had never been used by the Arabs before, but now Muhammad had entered the world.

Nurses from the desert came to Mecca to find babies to look after. It was normal for rich city families to give their babies to women from the desert to take care of. Both families gained from this custom—the desert family received gifts and good treatment from the baby's father, and the child was brought up in the clean desert environment, away from pollution and sicknesses. What's more, everybody liked the Bedouin from the desert because of their strong, independent character and the way they spoke the beautiful Arabic language. The city families wanted their children to learn this traditional culture.

One of the nurses was Halima, a poor woman from the tribe of Bani Saad. The Quraysh, the rich ruling tribe in Mecca, didn't want to give any of their babies to Halima because they were worried about trusting such a poor woman with their children, and none of the other nurses wanted to take Muhammad because they knew that, as his father had died, they would not receive anything in return. Having no other choice, Halima took Muhammad.

Halima would later explain how her life had changed completely when she began to look after the boy. "As soon as I stepped out into the desert with Muhammad," she would say, "we began to receive gifts from God. Whenever our sheep went out to the fields, they would return full of milk, even though the sheep of my fellow Bedouin came back hungry and with very little milk."

After spending several years with Halima, it was finally time for Muhammad to return to his mother. Halima didn't want him to go and held him close as she said goodbye.

When Muhammad was six years old, his mother, Amina, took him to Yathrib, an oasis 200 miles north of Mecca, to visit family members. On the way back to Mecca, Amina became sick and died.

So Abd al-Muttalib decided to raise his grandson, always showering him with love. However, Muhammad's happiness was not to last. Two years after of his mother died, Muhammad's grandfather also died. Muhammad was left in the care of his uncle, Abu Talib, who was a respected member of the Quraysh. Muhammad moved to Abu Talib's house, where his uncle and his aunt, Fatima, were very kind to him and treated him as one of their own children.

When Muhammad was twelve, Abu Talib

agreed to take him on a business trip to Syria. On their way, they passed a place where a Christian monk called Bahira lived all alone. It was unusual for Bahira to watch travelers, but he saw them going through the desert and invited them to stop. When he met Muhammad, he saw that here was the prophet who had been described in the Christian books. He looked at Muhammad's back and saw, as he was expecting, the apple-shaped mark that was the sign that Muhammad was special.

"Great things will happen to this boy!" he cried.

He told Abu Talib not to continue the trip, and return with Muhammad to Mecca, where he should take very good care of him.

By the time Muhammad was twenty-five, everybody called him "al-Amin," which means "the trustworthy." He had been working as a trader for several years, and it was clear that he was very different from everyone around him.

He was always honest and fair in business, and never used dirty tricks, which were all too common at the time. Muhammad was thoughtful, kind and polite.

One of the merchants in Mecca was a rich woman called Khadija. She had had two husbands, and being an experienced trader herself, she now had men who worked for her in the trading business. She had heard good things about "al-Amin," so chose him as a person she could trust to sell some goods for her in Syria. Khadija sent her servant Maysara to Syria with Muhammad, and when they returned, Maysara reported that al-Amin really was a most excellent person.

Khadija was an intelligent and noble woman. She thought very hard about Muhammad, this very honest man with his thick, curly hair and beard, and remembered the way his face always seemed to have a special glow. She decided to ask him to marry her.

Muhammad was surprised when she asked

him, but he was very pleased. They were married and had six children—Qasim, Zaynab, Ruqayya, Umm Kulthum, Fatima and Abdullah. They were a happy family, though there were also sad times, as both Qasim and Abdullah died while they were still small.

At that time, most of the people of Arabia believed in many gods. There was the High God, al-Lah, and there were also many lesser gods, such as al-Lat, al-Uzza and Manat. Idols had been put around the Kaaba, the shrine that Abraham had once built for people to pray to the one true God. People came from all over to pray and make offerings to the idols there.

Muhammad was sure that doing these things was wrong.

"How can a person worship a lifeless stone that can't help or hurt anyone?" he asked.

When Muhammad was thirty-five years old,

there was a large flood in Mecca. It damaged many of the houses and the Kaaba. The Quraysh decided that each group of families should be given a part of the Kaaba to rebuild so that they could all help with the important work. When they were about to put the sacred Black Stone in its special place, a big argument began about who would have the honor of putting it in.

As the angry voices got louder and louder, a Quraysh noble had an idea. "Let's ask the first man who comes through the gate what to do."

They all agreed. A person appeared.

"Oh! It's Muhammad the trustworthy! We'll do whatever he decides!" they said.

Muhammad listened carefully to the reasons for their argument, and asked for a cloak. He put it on the ground and put the Black Stone in the middle of it.

"Each group must hold onto an edge of the cloak," he explained calmly, "and all shall carry it together."

In this way, everybody carried the Black Stone, and Muhammad placed it in its final position himself.

Muhammad began to leave the busy city of Mecca sometimes to go into the mountains; he wanted to get away from the excitement and noise of town life and be closer to God. He would take a little food and drink with him, which he gave to poor people who visited him.

He thought deeply about how much he hated the way that the Quraysh prayed to so many gods and idols. It was very different from how he felt people's relationship with God should be. He also worried about the way the people around him lived their lives. There was too much fighting between the different tribes, and everybody seemed to be desperate to get money and power, even if they had to hurt the weakest people, including widows and orphans.

When he was forty years old, in the month

of Ramadan, which is the ninth month of the lunar year, Muhammad climbed high up into the mountains above Mecca, to the cave of Hira. One night he had been meditating and had fallen asleep. Suddenly the angel Gabriel appeared and commanded, "Recite!"

Muhammad was very surprised to see the angel. "But I cannot recite," he answered.

The angel Gabriel held Muhammad so tightly that he felt he couldn't take it any longer. Then the angel let go of him and repeated, "Recite!"

Muhammad repeated, "I cannot recite."

The angel held him tightly once again until Muhammad felt that he was close to death. Then the angel let go of him a second time, commanding, "Recite in the name of your Lord, who created man from a clinging substance. Recite, for your Lord is most generous, and taught by the pen, teaching man that which he knew not."

By this time Muhammad was shivering and

afraid. It was difficult for him to stand up and walk away from the front of the cave. When Khadija saw him, she could tell how upset he was. It was as if he had a fever.

"What's the matter?" she asked, reaching out to him. "Where have you been?"

"Cover me! Cover me!" he begged her.

Khadija put a cloak on him and held him closely, wondering what had happened.

When Muhammad was able to relax a little, he told her what he had seen and heard, and how afraid he had been. "Don't be afraid," said Khadija. "You are a good man. God will never let you down."

Khadija had the idea of asking the opinion of her cousin Waraqa, a wise Christian who knew a lot about holy scriptures. When Waraqa heard the story, he got a bit smile on his face. He told Khadija what she was already thinking: Muhammad had seen the angel of revelation — therefore he must be a prophet!

Khadija was the first person to believe

that Muhammad brought a message from God, and she was the first Muslim. She gave Muhammad strength and support, and helped him in every way she could for the rest of her life.

After that day, Muhammad received many messages from the angel Gabriel, together with the divine power to recite them. The verses were gathered together and became the Qur'an, the holy book of the Muslims.

God told Muhammad that there was only one God, the same God that Abraham had prayed to. He explained that all human beings should surrender themselves to God, which meant that He was more important than anything else in their lives, even money and fame. He told Muhammad that everyone is equal before God — men, women, rich people and poor people, and it makes no difference which family you come from. When people die they are judged for what they have done during their

lives, so it is very important that they be good
and do good things to everyone else, especially
those who are weaker and poorer than them.

God told Muhammad that Muslims should
stay close to God through regular prayers. The
angel Gabriel showed Muhammad how Muslims should pray, and how they should wash in
a special way before saying their prayers.

Muhammad shared the teachings with the
people who were closest to him. To begin with
Khadija prayed with him, and they were soon
joined by their daughters, Zaynab, Ruqayya,
Umm Kulthum and Fatima. Ali, Abu Talib's
son, whom Muhammad was bringing up, also
joined them, as did Zayd, a young man who
had been Muhammad's slave. Umm Ayman,
one of Muhammad's nurses from when he
was a child, came to pray, as did Abu Bakr,
Muhammad's closest friend. Thus Muhammad began to share the teachings of God with
those he could trust.

Abu Bakr was a popular businessman in

Mecca, and people often came to talk to him. "Have you heard that Muhammad is the Prophet of God?" he asked them. "The angel Gabriel came to Muhammad to tell him that God has power over everything in our lives, and we mustn't ever forget that. When we die, our money and the things that we own can't help us. We must look after everybody who needs help. Then God will make us happy after we die."

The new Muslims met in secret to pray and learn from Muhammad about the new religion. They were men and women from all the different clans. Some of them were rich, but many of them were poor and had been treated badly by those around them. They liked the idea that everybody was equal before God, and that the weaker people should be helped.

After three years, Muhammad received a message from God telling him to share the new religion with everyone. He climbed up to the top of Mount Safa and shouted out the names of all the nobles. Thinking there was a great danger in the city, everybody quickly came together at the bottom of the mountain.

"If I were to warn you that there were men on horses in the valley about to attack you, would you believe me?" he called down to them.

"Yes," they replied together. "We have never heard you lie."

"I have been ordered to warn you that terrible things will happen to you if you do not believe in the one God!" he cried out, his voice filling the whole area.

There was a second of silence. Then Abu Lahab, one of the important men in the crowd, shouted out angrily, "Lies! Did you really gather us here to tell us this nonsense?"

Abu Lahab walked through the crowd, his face red. The people in the crowd did not know what to do. Who were they supposed to believe? They started to walk away.

Muhammad was left alone. How would he ever make people believe his message from God?

Muhammad and the Muslims now began to teach openly, calling their message Islam, or "submission." They told the people that the gods and idols of the old religion weren't real. This made the leaders of the Quraysh angrier and angrier. The idols in the Kaaba brought many visitors to Mecca, and the money these visitors spent there made some people rich. If Muhammad made everybody believe that the idols were worthless, the Quraysh would lose money and power.

The leaders of the Quraysh visited Abu Talib several times to order him to force his nephew to stop trying to teach people about what God wanted. Abu Talib tried to talk with Muhammad to find a way to make things better, but when he realized that Muhammad would never stop trying to share the new religion, he gave up. Instead he promised that he would always protect him, even though he didn't want to become a Muslim himself.

Some Muslims who didn't belong to powerful families were attacked by people who wanted them to stop following the new religion and to scare other people so they would not join it. The first person to die because she was a Muslim was called Sumayya.

Muhammad hated to see these things happening to Muslims. He made a secret plan for two groups of them to go by boat to Abyssinia, where there was a Christian king who was well known for being kind and fair. When the leaders of the Quraysh learned that some of the Muslims had left, they were very, very angry. They quickly sent men with gifts to Abyssinia to convince the king to send the Muslims back, but the king, on hearing a verse from the Qur'an about Jesus and his mother Mary, wiped tears from his eyes and told the Muslims that they didn't have to go back to Mecca. They could stay in Abyssinia and live in peace.

The Quraysh tried to upset Muhammad and make his life miserable many times, often by doing mean little things like putting thorns on the path where he was about to walk. One day, Abu Jahl, a leader of the Quraysh, shouted out bad things about Islam as he passed Muhammad. Muhammad did not listen to him and looked the other way. Hamza, Muhammad's uncle, was the strongest man in the Quraysh at the time. He wasn't a Muslim, but he did respect Muhammad. That day he had been hunting, and was walking on the street with his bow and arrow when a woman called out to him to tell him about the bad things Abu Jahl had said. Hamza quickly became very angry. He ran off to find Abu Jahl, and when he found him, he hit him hard with his bow. "How dare you insult Muhammad's religion, when I also follow it."

Hamza's hatred of disrespect and his wanting to support his nephew led him to join Islam there and then.

Hearing the shouting, people gathered around to help Abu Jahl. Holding his head, he said, "Leave Hamza alone; I admit that I did say very bad things to his nephew."

When Hamza joined the Muslims, it made them much stronger. The Quraysh knew that Hamza would try to protect Muhammad, so they stopped saying so many bad things to him.

Umar ibn al-Khattab was another man in Mecca at the time whom many people were afraid of, and was also very well respected. He had wanted to kill Muhammad, but when he heard verses of the Qur'an, he became a Muslim.

Now that Hamza and Umar were on their side, the Muslims began to pray openly at the Kaaba.

When they found that they couldn't make Muhammad give up his teaching by insulting him and threatening him, the Quraysh were very unhappy. The Muslims wouldn't stop believing in their new religion, even when people attacked them. They didn't even fight back. They continued to pray, and to say that they believed that there was only one God and that Muhammad was God's Messenger.

"The only thing we can do is to make the Muslims so hungry and isolated that they will want to return to the old ways," the Quraysh thought.

So a notice was put up at the Kaaba saying that everybody had to stay away from the Muslims and Muhammad's group, and that nobody could trade with them. The Muslims became hungrier and hungrier, and poorer and poorer.

Finally, after two long years, some of the Muslims' family members were able to end the boycott. When they went to the Kaaba to tear down the notice they found that all the words on it had been eaten by worms, except for "In Your Name, O God."

Muhammad was happy to be able to live and trade normally again, but it suddenly came to an end. Khadija, his dear wife, died. She had always helped him to have confidence in himself and his work of teaching people about God's teachings, but now he would have to continue by himself.

Several months later, Abu Talib also died. Muhammad felt very sad because he had lost his kind uncle, who had always tried to protect him, even though they didn't have the same ideas about God.

Muhammad and the Muslims were now in more danger than ever before. They didn't have Abu Talib stopping the Quraysh from harming them. People threw dirt in Muhammad's face, and he wondered how long it would be before they did worse.

Muhammad decided that it was time to share the message from God with people outside Mecca. He went to the green and beautiful town of Taif and spoke there about Islam, but nobody wanted to listen. People even threw stones at him.

Muhammad felt very, very sad. He found a quiet place and prayed to God. He didn't understand all the terrible things that were happening to the Muslims, but he trusted that God was in control of his life and would choose what was best for him in the end.

Soon after, something happened that made Muhammad feel a little better. He had returned to Mecca, and he went to sleep near the Kaaba. Then he saw the angel Gabriel next to him and the angel showed him a most magnificent white beast with wings.

"This is Buraq," the angel Gabriel told Muhammad.

Muhammad climbed on Buraq, and with

the angel next to him he found himself taken out of Mecca, high across the Arabian Peninsula, and north to the city of Jerusalem. The long trip that would usually have taken weeks took just a few moments.

They arrived at Jerusalem's great al-Aqsa mosque. There Muhammad met the prophets who had come before him—Abraham, Moses and Jesus and more—and led them in prayer. He understood that he was the last in the long line of prophets.

Then Muhammad went up on Buraq again, and the angel Gabriel led them from the mosque up through the clouds, higher and higher, until they had passed through all the heavens. Muhammad finally met God, who told Muhammad that it was important that all Muslims should pray five times every day.

Buraq then carried Muhammad back to Mecca. Amazingly it was still nighttime when they arrived.

The Night Journey to Jerusalem and the

Ascension to the Heavens gave Muhammad great comfort and a relaxed feeling. It showed that he was a prophet who belonged with the greatest prophets of the past. It gave him new energy after the long months of hard, lonely times.

Every year pilgrims from all over the Arab countries traveled to the Kaaba in Mecca. Some pilgrims from the city of Yathrib had heard about Muhammad and his new religion, and when they came to Mecca, they asked him about it. They quickly found out that he really was the Messenger of God, and became Muslims. They explained that the fighting between the tribes around Yathrib was destroying them. Perhaps, they thought, God had sent Muhammad to bring the tribes together again.

Two years later, more people from Yathrib came to speak to Muhammad. They met in secret at night on a hill called Aqaba. In the moonlight the leaders from Yathrib told Muhammad that if he and the Meccan Muslims came to Yathrib, the people of Yathrib would be loyal to Muhammad and protect him and the Muslims.

Muhammad replied, "I am yours and you are mine. I will fight anybody that you fight. I will make peace with anybody you make peace with."

At last Muhammad and the Muslims were no longer alone.

During the summer of that year the Muslims began quietly to leave Mecca to go to live in Yathrib. Before long all Muhammad's closest followers had gone except for Abu Bakr and Ali, who stayed with Muhammad in Mecca.

The Quraysh had been becoming more and more worried that Muhammad was getting too much power, and they called a meeting to talk about how to stop him. They wanted to kill him. Abu Jahl thought of a plan. A young, powerful member from each clan should attack Muhammad at exactly the same moment. At that time the law said that when one person murdered another, the clan of the victim would seek revenge on the tribe of the murderer. But if all the men killed Muhammad at the very same time, Muhammad's group wouldn't be able to attack *all* the others. In this way they would be able to kill Muhammad without putting themselves in danger.

When it became night, the young people gathered outside Muhammad's house and waited for him to leave for the morning prayer. One of them looked and saw a sleeping person covered in Muhammad's green cloak.

He returned to the others and whispered, "Muhammad is inside, and he's sleeping. He'll be out soon."

But when the morning came, nobody had left the house. Suddenly the door opened. The people all had their weapons ready. But it was

Ali, not Muhammad. Muhammad had gotten out during the night without any of them seeing him.

Muhammad had gone quickly to Abu Bakr's house, and the two of them had gone together into the mountains. They knew that as soon as the Quraysh found out that Muhammad had left Mecca, they would do their best to find him and kill him. They waited in a cave in the mountain of Thawr to the south of Mecca.

Abu Bakr's son, Abdullah, came to them with news of what was being said about them in Mecca, and his daughter Asma brought them food.

Three days later Muhammad and Abu Bakr heard some of the Quraysh looking for them near the cave. "They're very close," said Abu Bakr in a quiet voice. "If one of them turns around now, he'll see us."

Muhammad was not afraid. "Don't worry," he told his friend. "God is with us."

The Quraysh saw that there was a cave and went to look at it. When they got near, they saw that a spider had made its web over the front of the cave and two doves had built nests in front of it. They all agreed that no one could be inside this cave, and moved on.

Once they were sure that it was safe to come out, Muhammad and Abu Bakr found their camels again and set out once more for Yathrib.

They were sure that the Quraysh would be watching carefully on the easy road from Mecca to Yathrib, so, using a guide who was not a Muslim but was well known for being honest, they set off southwest, away from Yathrib. When they felt safe enough, they turned to the north and went beside the sea, back towards Yathrib. The Quraysh never imagined that they would choose such an unusual route, so they did not find them.

Muhammad's journey from Mecca to Yathrib became known as the Hijra, and the year in which it took place, 622 of the Christian calendar, became Year 1 of the Muslim calendar.

Many people were excited when Muhammad arrived in Yathrib. There were songs and cries of "God is great!" Everybody wanted him to stay with them. He didn't want it to seem that he liked one family better than another, so he let go of the reins of his camel and said that he would live wherever it chose.

Everybody watched with excitement as the animal went through the streets. After some time it came to some land where there was a barn used for drying dates. This was where Muhammad chose to build his home and a mosque. Both were built very simply, as Muhammad believed that money should not be spent on expensive goods, but on helping the poor. The mosque was used for prayer and also for meetings. People of all religions and from all tribes would come and talk to

Muhammad about their problems, and he would give them advice.

The city of Yathrib became known as Medina, a short form of Medinat al-Nabi, or "the city of the Prophet." When the Muslims and Muhammad came to Medina, they called their new community the "umma." The relationships in Medina between people of different religions and tribes needed to be clear, so Muhammad made rules that made everybody's rights and duties clear. Muslims would be judged using the laws of Islam, and non-Muslims would be judged using their own laws and would be free to continue with their own religions. However, if the Muslims or the people on their side were attacked, everybody had a duty to join together to protect each other.

The Muslims prayed five times a day, and as the times of these prayers depended on the position of the sun in the sky, which changed throughout the year, they needed to be told just before each prayer time. They held a meeting and decided that there should be a special loud call to prayer across the city. Muhammad gave the honor of being the first person to call Muslims to prayer to Bilal, a freed black slave who had suffered greatly in Mecca for being a Muslim.

After Khadija's death, Muhammad married several wives, as was normal at the time. His favorite of these was Abu Bakr's daughter, Aisha. She was intelligent and lively, and she wasn't afraid to ask questions or tell others what she thought. She carefully watched what Muhammad did, and she remembered what he told her about Islam and his life. Muhammad trusted Aisha so much that he said that Muslims should learn half their religious knowledge from her.

Aisha would continue to teach people about the things Muhammad said and did long after he had died. Muslims used this information to help them decide what God wanted them to do in life.

Most of Muhammad's other wives were widows of Muslims who had died fighting for Islam, and women from other tribes. By marrying them, he created strong links between the Muslims and the other tribes. His wives lived in small huts attached to the mosque so they were at the center of the community, and would often talk about things that were happening with him.

Some parts of the Qur'an said that women had the same religious rights and responsibilities as men, and that they should receive their own inheritance, which had not happened before.

Although the Muslims were now safe in Medina, they needed to get power again in Mecca if Islam was to become a strong religion for everybody, not just for those in the city of Medina.

They thought about how best to make the Quraysh's power in Mecca weaker. One way would be to attack the Quraysh's caravans traveling between Mecca and Syria.

Abu Sufyan, the head of the Quraysh, was traveling with a large caravan from Syria to Mecca when he was told that the Muslims were planning to attack it. He asked the Quraysh in Mecca for help. The caravan made it safely to Mecca, but the Quraysh had sent an army of a thousand men to attack the Muslims. The Muslims gathered just over three hundred men and a battle began near the wells of Badr. After fierce fighting, the Muslims won, not losing many of their own men, but killing a great many of the Quraysh, including Abu Jahl.

Muhammad divided the things the Muslims got from the fight fairly between everyone. He said that all prisoners must be well looked after. The poor ones could become Muslims or be sent back to Mecca; the rich ones could join Islam or, if some money was paid, they could return to Mecca.

The Muslims returned to Medina. They were very happy because they had won against an army that was much larger than theirs. The Quraysh returned to Mecca deeply embarrassed by such a defeat. What should they do now? Should they simply accept the death of so many of their heroes?

Early the next year the Muslims heard that the Quraysh were getting ready to fight them again. The two sides met at Uhud. The Muslims waited just in front of the mountain so they could not be attacked from behind. Muhammad put archers on the top of the hill. He said they had to stay there and fight even if it was very dangerous. Again there were many more warriors from the Quraysh than there were Muslims, but the Muslims fought hard and looked like the Quraysh were about to lose.

The archers thought they were going to win, so they moved from the top of the mountain to try to get things from the enemy. But Quraysh men on horses suddenly attacked the Muslims. There was great confusion and many Muslims were killed, including Hamza, Muhammad's uncle. Most of the others lost hope and ran away.

Just a few people stayed with Muhammad, who had been hurt. Among these was Nusayba, a woman who had been bringing water to the Muslim fighters. When she saw Muhammad, she took a sword and began to defend him. Muhammad saw that she had no shield, so she shouted to one of the men who was running away, "Give your shield to the one who is fighting!"

The man threw it to Nusayba and she continued with her sword, hitting the enemy again and again. However, she was attacked by men on horses and received thirteen wounds, including one in her neck that took a year to heal.

The Quraysh won this time. The Muslims

returned to Medina. They were very sad about the loss of family and friends.

The next year the Quraysh marched towards the Muslims again. The Muslims decided to dig a trench along the edge of the city to stop the enemy from getting in. Everybody helped, including Muhammad himself.

When the Muslims' enemies saw the long, wide trench they did not know what to do. The Quraysh and those with them tried to cross the trench, but they couldn't find a way.

Then the Qurayzah, one of the Jewish tribes inside Medina that had been on the Muslims' side, decided to join with the enemies of the Muslims outside the city. The Muslims, who could not leave their city for fear of attack, had almost run out of food, and now they had enemies both outside and within.

Muhammad prayed to God for something to change so that the Muslims would not all be killed and the message of Islam lost.

A very big sandstorm blew up, and it lasted for days. The Quraysh didn't know what to do. Their animals were dying, their things were being damaged, and they couldn't make any food to eat. It was impossible to fight anymore, so they went back to Mecca.

Although the battle of Medina was over, the Muslims still had to do something about the Qurayzah, who had betrayed the Muslims. Muhammad said the Qurayzah could choose who would judge them, and they chose a man from the tribe of Aws who had always had a good relationship with the Qurayzah. He said that they had to be punished. All their men should be killed, all the women and children taken as prisoners, and all their things would be divided between the Muslims.

The Muslims in Medina wanted to visit the Kaaba. Muhammad and 1,400 Muslims left for Mecca. When the Quraysh heard about it, they were afraid that the Muslims would try to take the city if they got in.

The Muslims left Medina with no weapons, and traveled south towards Mecca. At the wells of Hudaybiyya they stopped and waited. Some of the Quraysh came out to meet them to talk about what should happen. The Treaty of Hudaybiyya was made. It was agreed that the Muslims would not be able to visit Mecca that year, but they could return the next year and safely visit the Kaaba. The treaty said there should be no war between the two groups for ten years, and that people should be free to choose to join either Muhammad and the Muslims, or with the Quraysh.

The Muslims had written into the treaty the words "Muhammad, Prophet of God," but the Quraysh said that it should say, "Muhammad, son of Abdullah." The Muslims were very angry about this, but Muhammad said it was not important. Words did not have to be written on paper for them to be true.

Muhammad also told them that the Qur'an taught that if the Muslims' enemies said they would accept peace, the Muslims always had to agree. Peace was always better than war.

Later that day, God revealed a new part of the Qur'an that showed that the treaty had been a great victory for the Muslims. They had shown that not only did they have a strong faith, but also that they were humble and calm, showed mercy and could control themselves.

According to the Treaty of Hudaybiyya, there could be no fighting for ten years. However, soon after the treaty was signed the tribe of Bakr, who were on the Quraysh side, attacked the tribe of Khuza'a, who were on the Muslim side. The Quraysh helped the tribe of Bakr, and this broke the treaty.

Muhammad now went to Mecca with the largest army of Muslims ever. The Quraysh were afraid. They had spent thirteen years insulting and hurting the Muslims when they were living in Mecca, and they had spent eight years fighting the Muslims after they had moved to Medina. Now they had broken an important treaty, how would the Muslims behave?

The large Muslim army entered Mecca and took control of the city peacefully. Muhammad put up his red tent near the Kaaba. He walked around and thanked God sincerely for the Muslims' great win. He then called the people of Mecca together.

"O Quraysh," he cried. "What do you think I should do with you?"

"We hope for the best," they said. "You are a noble brother."

"Go your own ways!" said Muhammad. "You are all free now." He had decided that the Quraysh should be forgiven for what they had done to the Muslims in the past. Many decided to become Muslims, but they did not have to.

The Muslims were very happy that they were finally able to pray at the Kaaba again. They destroyed the idols the Quraysh had prayed to so the shrine would once again only be for the one true God.

When the Muslims arrived in Mecca, some people were not happy about it. The Muslims continued to fight to make sure that they remained powerful. More and more people chose to become Muslims, and more and more tribes traveled to Medina to swear that they would be loyal to Muhammad.

Ten years after the Hijra, Muhammad decided to lead the hajj, the official pilgrimage to Mecca that every able Muslim has to make. Muhammad showed the Muslims what they should do on their trip, and explained to them the meaning of each action.

He called all the Muslims together near Mount Arafat. The crowd was very large, and everybody hoped to see Muhammad. By now he was an old man, and he knew that this would probably be his last chance to speak to so many Muslims in this way. When the crowd was quiet, Muhammad began to talk.

He reminded them of everything that Islam had taught them, that they should praise God, be kind and fair to everyone and not fight each other. "Have I faithfully delivered my message to you?" he asked.

"Yes, you have!" the crowd shouted, and their voices rolled around the valley.

Two months later Muhammad fell ill. He died in Aisha's arms, and was buried near her house. He had spent the last twenty-three years teaching people to believe in the one true God, to put their trust in Him, and to understand that He was more important than anything else. Muhammad had taught people that they would be rewarded or punished for their actions in this life. Everybody is equal before God, and it makes no difference whether they are men or women, what color they are, which family they belong to, or how rich or poor they are. The only way one person can be better than another is by loving God more, and by showing this love in the way they live their life.

Word List

A

- **a** 冠 ①1つの，1人の，ある ②～につき **a bit** わずか，少し **a lot of** たくさんの～ **a sort of** ～のようなもの，一種の～

- **Abd al-Muttalib** アブド・アル・ムッタリブ《ムハンマドの父方の祖父》

- **abdicate** 動 (王位・地位などを) 捨てる，放棄する

- **Abdullah** 名 ①アブドゥッラーフ《ムハンマドの父》②アブドゥッラーフ《ムハンマドの息子》

- **able** 形 ①《be - to ～》(人が) ～することができる ②能力のある

- **about** 副 ①およそ，約 ②まわりに，あたりを **be about to** まさに～しようとしている，～するところだ 前 ①～について ②～のまわりに[の]

- **above** 前 ①～の上に，～より上で，～以上で ③～を超えて 副 ①上に ②以上に 形 上記の 名《the -》上記の人[こと]

- **Abraham** 名 イブラーヒーム (アブラハム)《ノアの洪水後，神による人類救済の出発点として選ばれ祝福された最初の預言者》

- **absent** 形 不在の，欠けた，欠席[欠

勤]した

- **Abu Bakr** アブー・バクル (・アッ＝スィッディーク)《ムハンマドの最初の友人》

- **Abu Jahl** アブー・ジャハル《ムハンマドを迫害していたクライシュ族の頭目》

- **Abu Lahab** アブー・ラハブ《ムハンマドの父方の叔父でクライシュ族の指導者の一人》

- **Abu Sufyan** アブー・スフヤーン《マッカのクライシュ族の指導者であり商人》

- **Abu Talib** アブー＝ターリブ《ムハンマドの叔父であり育ての親》

- **Abyssinia** 名 アビシニア《エチオピアの旧称》

- **accept** 動 ①受け入れる ②同意する，認める

- **according** 副《- to ～》～によれば[よると]

- **accuse** 動《- of ～》～ (の理由) で告訴[非難]する

- **achieve** 動 成し遂げる，達成する，成功を収める

- **across** 前 ～を渡って，～の向こう側に，(身体の一部に) かけて **go across** 横断する，渡る

- □ **act** 動 行動する
- □ **action** 名 ①行動, 活動 ②動作, 行為
- □ **admit** 動 認める, 許可する, 入れる
- □ **advice** 名 忠告, 助言, 意見
- □ **advise** 動 忠告する, 勧める
- □ **afraid** 形 ①心配して ②恐れて, こわがって **be afraid of** ～を恐れる, ～を怖がる
- □ **after** 前 ①～の後に [で], ～の次に ②《前後に名詞がきて》次々に～, 何度も～《反復・継続を表す》**after a while** しばらくして **after all** やはり, 結局 副 後に [で] **look after** ～の世話をする, ～に気をつける
- □ **afternoon** 名 午後
- □ **again** 副 再び, もう一度 **again and again** 何度も繰り返して
- □ **against** 前 ～に対して, ～に反対して, (規則など) に違反して
- □ **age** 名 年齢 **old age** 老齢
- □ **aging** 名 老化, 高齢化
- □ **ago** 副 ～前に **long ago** ずっと前に, 昔
- □ **agree** 動 ①同意する ②意見が一致する
- □ **ahead** 副 ①前方へ [に] ②前もって ③進歩して, 有利に **go ahead** 先に行く, 《許可を表す》どうぞ
- □ **Ahimsaka** 名 アヒンサカ《アングリマーラの本名》
- □ **air** 名 《the-》空中, 空間 **open air** 戸外, 野外
- □ **Aisha** 名 アーイシャ《・ビント・アブー・バクル》《アブー・バクルの娘でムハンマドの3番目の妻》
- □ **Ajatasatru** 名 アジャータシャトル, 阿闍世 (あじゃせ)《マガダ国の王》
- □ **al-Amin** 名 アル・アミン《商人だったころのムハンマドの通り名。Aminは「正直, 信頼性の高い」の意味》
- □ **al-Aqsa mosque** アル=アクサー・モスク《エルサレムの旧市街にあるイスラム最初期につくられたモスクのひとつ》
- □ **al-Lah** 名 アッラーー《イスラム教の唯一神》
- □ **al-Lat** 名 アッラート《イスラム教以前の時代に崇められていた女神》
- □ **al-Uzza** 名 アル・ウッザー《イスラム教以前の時代に崇められていた女神》
- □ **Alara Kalama** アーラーラ・カーラーマ, 阿羅邏迦蘭 (あららからん)《思想家。釈迦が出家後に最初に師事した人物の1人》
- □ **Ali** 名 アリー (・イブン・アビー・ターリブ)《アブー=ターリブの息子》
- □ **alive** 形 生きている
- □ **all** 形 すべての, ～中 **all night long** 一晩中 **all one's life** ずっと, 生まれてから **all over** ～中で, 全体に亘って, ～の至る所で **all the time** ずっと, いつも, その間ずっと **with all one's heart** 心から 代 全部, すべて (のもの [人]) 名 全体 **after all** やはり, 結局
- □ **all-** 形 全体の, 全ての, 最高の, あらゆる
- □ **almost** 副 ほとんど, もう少しで (～するところ)
- □ **alms** 名 施し物〈古〉
- □ **alone** 形 ただひとりの 副 ひとりで, ～だけで **leave ～ alone** ～をそっとしておく
- □ **along** 前 ～に沿って **along the way** 途中で, これまでに, この先
- □ **already** 副 すでに, もう
- □ **also** 副 ～も (また), ～も同様に 接 その上, さらに
- □ **alternative** 名 2つのうちの1つ, 代替え手段, 代替案
- □ **although** 接 ～だけれども, ～にもかかわらず, たとえ～でも
- □ **always** 副 いつも, 常に **not always** 必ずしも～であるとは限らない

133

□ **am** 動 ～である，（～に）いる［ある］《主語がIのときのbeの現在形》

□ **amazing** 形 驚くべき，見事な

□ **amazingly** 副 驚いたことに

□ **Amina** 名 アーミナ《ムハンマドの母》

□ **among** 前 （3つ以上のもの）の間で［に］，～の中で［に］

□ **amongst** 前 の間に［を・で］

□ **an** 冠 ①1つの，1人の，ある ②～につき

□ **Ananda** 名 アーナンダ 阿難陀，阿難（あなん）《釈迦の十大弟子の一人》

□ **anapana sati** アーナーパーナ・サティ，安那般那念（あんなはんなねん）《呼吸を軸としてこれを念じつつ，身心そして法を観察して悟りにいたらんとする，仏教の瞑想法の一つ》

□ **Anathapindika** 名 アナータピンディカ，給孤独（ぎっこどく）《本名はスダッタ，須達多，須達（しゅだつ）。コーサラ国首都シュラーヴァスティー（舎衛城）の長者。祇園精舎を建てた》

□ **and** 接 ①そして，～と… ②《同じ語を結んで》ますます ③《結果を表して》それで，だから **and so** そこで，それだから，それで

□ **Andrew** 名 アンデレ《十二使徒の一人》

□ **angel** 名 ①天使 ②天使のような人 **angel of revelation** 啓示の天使《神のことばを伝える天使》

□ **anger** 名 怒り

□ **angrily** 副 怒って，腹立たしげに

□ **angry** 形 怒って，腹を立てて

□ **Angulimala** 名 アングリマーラ，央掘摩羅（おうくつまら）《釈迦の弟子の一人》

□ **animal** 名 動物

□ **ankle** 名 足首

□ **Anoma, River** アノマ川《ネパール南部のカピラヴァストゥ近くの川》

□ **another** 形 ①もう1つ［1人］の ②別の 代 ①もう1つ［1人］ ②別のもの

□ **another Simon** 熱心党のシモン《十二使徒の一人》

□ **answer** 動 答える，応じる 名 答え，応答，返事 **in answer to** ～に応じて

□ **any** 形 ①《疑問文で》何か，いくつかの ②《否定文で》何も，少しも（～ない） ③《肯定文で》どの～も **any time** いつでも **not ～ any longer** もはや～でない［～しない］ 代 ①《疑問文で》（～のうち）何か，どれか，誰か ②《否定文で》少しも，何も［誰も］～ない ③《肯定文で》どれも，誰でも **if any** もしあれば，あったとしても

□ **anybody** 代 ①《疑問文・条件節で》誰か ②《否定文で》誰も（～ない） ③《肯定文で》誰でも

□ **anymore** 副 《通例否定文，疑問文で》今はもう，これ以上，これから

□ **anyone** 代 ①《疑問文・条件節で》誰か ②《否定文で》誰も（～ない） ③《肯定文で》誰でも

□ **anything** 代 ①《疑問文で》何か，どれでも ②《否定文で》何も，どれも（～ない） ③《肯定文で》何でも，どれでも **anything else** ほかの何か 副 いくらか

□ **apostle** 名 使徒

□ **appear** 動 ①現れる，見えてくる ②（～のように）見える，～らしい

□ **apple** 名 リンゴ

□ **apple-shaped** 形 リンゴの形をした

□ **Aqaba** 名 アカバ《マッカ郊外の地名》

□ **Arab** 名 アラビア人，アラブ民族，アラブ 形 アラブ（人）の

□ **Arabia** 名 アラビア，アラブ

□ **Arabian Peninsula** アラビア半島

□ **Arabic** 形 アラビアの

WORD LIST

□ **Arafat, Mount** アラファト山《マッカ東方にある花崗岩でできた山》

□ **archer** 图 弓の射手

□ **are** 動 ～である，(～に)いる[ある]《主語がyou, we, theyまたは複数名詞のときのbeの現在形》

□ **area** 图 地域，地方，区域，場所

□ **argue** 動 ①論じる，議論する ②主張する

□ **argument** 图 ①議論，論争 ②論拠，理由

□ **arm** 图 腕

□ **armed** 形 武装した

□ **army** 图 軍隊

□ **around** 前 ～のまわりに，～のあちこちに 副 ①まわりに，あちこちに ②およそ，約 **go around** 動き回る，あちらこちらに行く，回り道をする，(障害)を回避する **look around** まわりを見回す **move around** ～をあちこち動かす **turn around** 振り向く，向きを変える，方向転換する **walk around** 歩き回る，ぶらぶら歩く

□ **arrest** 動 逮捕する

□ **arrive** 動 到着する，到達する

□ **arrow** 图 矢，矢のようなもの

□ **as** 接 ①《as ～ as …の形で》…と同じくらい～ ②～のとおりに，～のように ③～しながら，～しているときに ④～するにつれて，～にしたがって ⑤～なので ⑥～だけれども ⑦～する限りでは 前 ①～として(の) ②～の時 副 同じくらい **as if** あたかも～のように，まるで～みたいに **as long as** ～する以上は，～である限りは **as many as** ～もの数の **as much as** ～と同じだけ **as soon as** ～するとすぐ，～するや否や **as well as** ～と同様に **as ～ as possible** できるだけ～ **be known as** ～として知られている **just as** (ちょうど)であろうとおり **see ～ as …** ～を…と考える **such as** たとえば～，～のような

□ **ascension** 图 上昇 **Ascension to the Heavens** 昇天

□ **ashamed** 形 恥ずかしく思う[恥じている]，～することに気が引ける

□ **Asita** 图 アシタ仙人，阿私仙，阿私陀《釈迦が将来，仏となると予言した》

□ **ask** 動 ①尋ねる，聞く ②頼む，求める

□ **asleep** 形 眠って(いる状態の) **fall asleep** 眠り込む，寝入る

□ **Asma** 图 アスマ《アブー・バクルの娘》

□ **astrologer** 图 占星術師

□ **at** 前 ①《場所・時》～に[で] ②《目標・方向》～に[を]，～に向かって ③《原因・理由》～を見て[聞いて・知って] ④～に従事して，～の状態で **at first** 最初は，初めのうちは **at home** 自宅で，在宅して **at last** ついに，とうとう **at that moment** その時に，その瞬間に **at that time** その時・その当時 **at the foot of** ～のすそ[下部]に **at the time** そのころ，当時は

□ **ate** 動 eat(食べる)の過去

□ **attach** 動 ①取り付ける，添える ②付随する，帰属する

□ **attached** 形 ついている，結びついた

□ **attack** 動 襲う，攻める

□ **attendant** 图 つき添い人

□ **attention** 图 注意，集中 **right attention** 正念(しょうねん)《正しい集中力》

□ **aunt** 图 おば

□ **authority** 图 権威，権力，権限

□ **avoid** 動 避ける，(～を)しないようにする

□ **awake** 形 目が覚めて

□ **awareness** 图 認識，自覚，意識性，気づいていること

□ **away** 形 離れた 副 離れて，遠くに，去って，わきに **be carried away** 我を忘れる，うっとりする **get away** 逃

135

げる, 逃亡する, 離れる **give away** ①
ただで与える, 贈る, 譲歩する, 手放
す ②（素性・正体を）暴露する, 馬脚
を現す **go away** 立ち去る **run away**
走り去る, 逃げ出す **stay away from**
〜から離れている **turn away** 向こう
へ行く, 追い払う,（顔を）そむける,
横を向く **walk away** 立ち去る, 遠ざ
かる

☐ **Aws** 图アウス族《ヤスリブに住ん
でいたアラブ人の有力部族》

☐ **axe** 图おの

B

☐ **baby** 图赤ん坊 **have a baby boy**
男の子を産む

☐ **back** 图①背中 ②裏, 後ろ 副①
戻って ②後ろへ［に］ **back to life**
生き返る, 息を吹き返す **come back**
戻る **fight back** 反撃に転じる, 応戦
する **go back to** 〜に帰る［戻る］,
〜に遡る,（中断していた作業に）再
び取り掛かる **turn back** 元に戻る
turn one's back on 〜に背中を向
ける, 〜を見捨てる 形裏の, 後ろの
動後ろへ動く, 後退する

☐ **bad** 形①悪い, へたな, まずい ②
気の毒な ③（程度が）ひどい, 激しい

☐ **badly** 副①悪く, まずく, へたに
②とても, ひどく

☐ **Badr** 图バドル《地名》

☐ **Bahira** 图バヒラ《キリスト教の修
道士。思春期のムハンマドに預言者と
しての将来を予言した》

☐ **Bakr** 图バクル族《マッカと同盟す
る遊牧民》

☐ **bamboo** 图竹（類）, 竹材

☐ **Bani Saad** バヌサアド族《ハリー
マの出身部族》

☐ **banyan tree** バンヤンツリー《イ
チジク属の樹木》

☐ **baptism** 图洗礼, バプテスマ

☐ **baptist** 图洗礼を授ける人

☐ **baptize** 動洗礼を施す, 清める

☐ **barber** 图理髪師, 床屋

☐ **barn** 图物置, 納屋

☐ **Bartholomew** 图バルトロマイ
《十二使徒の一人》

☐ **base** 图本部

☐ **bath** 图入浴, 水浴, 風呂

☐ **battle** 图戦闘, 戦い

☐ **BCE** 略西暦紀元前（before the
Common Era）

☐ **be** 動〜である,（〜に）いる［ある］,
〜となる 助①《現在分詞とともに用
いて》〜している ②《過去分詞とと
もに用いて》〜される, 〜されている

☐ **beard** 图あごひげ

☐ **beast** 图動物, けもの

☐ **beautiful** 形美しい, すばらしい

☐ **became** 動become（なる）の過去

☐ **because** 接（なぜなら）〜だから,
〜という理由で［原因］で **because of**
〜のために, 〜の理由で

☐ **become** 動①（〜に）なる ②
（〜に）似合う ③becomeの過去分詞

☐ **Bedouin** 图ベドウィン（族）《アラ
ブ系の遊牧民》

☐ **been** 動be（〜である）の過去分詞
助be（〜している・〜される）の過去
分詞

☐ **before** 前〜の前に［で］, 〜より以
前に **before long** やがて, まもなく
副以前に **the night before** 前の晩

☐ **beg** 動懇願する, お願いする

☐ **began** 動begin（始まる）の過去

☐ **beggar** 图乞食, 物貰い

☐ **begin** 動始まる［始める］, 起こる
to begin with はじめに, まず第一に

☐ **begun** 動begin（始まる）の過去分
詞

☐ **behave** 動振る舞う

☐ **behind** 前①〜の後ろに, 〜の背後

に ②〜に遅れて，〜に劣って 圖 ①
後ろに，背後に ②遅れて，劣って
leave behind あとにする，〜を置き
去りにする

□ **being** 图存在，生命，人間 **human
being** 人，人間

□ **believe** 働信じる，信じている，(〜
と) 思う，考える **believe in** 〜を信
じる

□ **belong** 働《- to 〜》〜に属する，
〜のものである

□ **beloved** 形最愛の，いとしい

□ **benefit** 働利益を得る，(〜の) ため
になる

□ **beside** 前 ①〜のそばに，〜と並ん
で ②〜と比べると ③〜とはずれて

□ **best** 形最もよい，最大 [多] の **do
one's best** 全力を尽くす **try one's
best** 全力を尽くす

□ **Bethany** 图ベタニア《エルサレム
近郊の地名》

□ **Bethsaida** 图ベッサイダ《ガリラ
ヤの町の名》

□ **betray** 働裏切る，背く，だます

□ **betrayal** 图裏切り，密告

□ **betrayer** 图裏切り者

□ **better** 形 ①よりよい ②(人が) 回
復して **feel better** 気分がよくなる
圖 ①よりよく，より上手に ②むしろ

□ **between** 前 (2つのもの) の間に
[で・の]

□ **beyond** 前〜を越えて，〜の向こ
うに

□ **Bhallika** 图バツリカ，跋梨迦《バ
クトリアから来た商人》

□ **bhikku** 图比丘 (びく)《出家し，具
足戒 (戒律の一種) を守る男性の修行
者》

□ **Bible** 图 ①《the -》聖書 ②《b-》権
威ある書物，バイブル

□ **big** 形大きい

□ **Bilal** 图ビラール (・ビン＝ラバー
フ・アル＝ハバシー)《アビシニア生

まれの黒人で元奴隷》

□ **Bimbisara** 图ビンビサーラ，頻婆
娑羅 (びんばしゃら)《マガダ国の王》

□ **bird** 图鳥

□ **birth** 图出産，誕生

□ **birthday** 图誕生日

□ **bit** 图《a -》少し，ちょっと

□ **black** 形黒い，有色の 图黒，黒色

□ **Black Stone** 黒石 (くろいし／こ
くせき)《カアバ神殿の東隅の外側，
地上から160センチメートルほどの
ところに据えられた黒い石》

□ **blasphemy** 图神への冒とく

□ **bleed** 働出血する，血を流す [流さ
せる]

□ **bless** 働神の加護を祈る，〜を祝福
する

□ **blessed** 形祝福された，恵まれた

□ **blessing** 图 ①(神の) 恵み，加護
②祝福の祈り ③(食前・食後の) 祈り

□ **blew** 働blow (吹く) の過去

□ **blood** 图血，血液

□ **blow** 働(風が) 吹く，(風が) 〜を吹
き飛ばす **blow up** 破裂する [させる]

□ **boat** 图ボート，小舟，船

□ **bodhi** 图ボーディー，菩提 (ぼだい)
《煩悩 (ぼんのう) を断ち切って悟り
の境地に達すること》

□ **Bodhi Tree** ゴータマ・ブッダの
菩提樹 (ぼだいじゅ)

□ **body** 图体，死体，胴体

□ **bone** 图骨，《-s》骨格

□ **book** 图本，書物

□ **border** 图境界，へり，国境

□ **born** 形生まれた，生まれながらの
be born 生まれる **be born into**
〜に生まれる

□ **both** 形両方の，2つとも 圖《both
〜 and … の形で》〜も…も両方とも
代両方，両者，双方 **both of them**
彼ら [それら] 両方とも

137

□ **bottom** 名底, 下部, すそ野, ふもと

□ **bought** 動 buy (買う) の過去, 過去分詞

□ **bow** 動 (〜に) お辞儀する 名弓, 弓状のもの

□ **bowl** 名どんぶり, わん, ボウル

□ **boy** 名少年, 男の子 **have a baby boy** 男の子を産む

□ **boycott** 名ボイコット, 集団排斥

□ **Brahma Sahampati** ブラフマー(梵天)・サハンパティ《仏教の天部の一尊で古代インドの神ブラフマーが仏教に取り入れられたもの》

□ **brahmin** 名バラモン, ブラフミン(婆羅門)《インドのカースト制度の頂点に位置する司祭階級》

□ **branch** 名枝

□ **bread** 名パン

□ **break** 動壊す, 折る **break through** 〜を打ち破る

□ **breath** 名息, 呼吸

□ **breathe** 動呼吸する

□ **breathing** 名呼吸, 息づかい

□ **brief** 形①短い時間の ②簡単な

□ **bright** 副輝いて, 明るく

□ **bring** 動①持ってくる, 連れてくる ②もたらす, 生じる **bring about** 引き起こす **bring up** ①育てる, 連れて行く ②(問題を)持ち出す

□ **broke** 動 break (壊す) の過去

□ **broken** 動 break (壊す) の過去分詞

□ **brother** 名兄弟

□ **brother-in-law** 名義理の兄弟

□ **brought** 動 bring (持ってくる) の過去, 過去分詞

□ **Buddha** 名ブッダ, 仏陀《古代インドの言葉で「目覚めた人」という意味》

□ **Buddhism** 名仏教, 仏道, 仏法

□ **Buddhist** 形仏教(徒)の, 仏陀の

名仏教徒

□ **build** 動建てる, 確立する

□ **built** 動 build (建てる) の過去, 過去分詞

□ **Buraq** 名ブラーク《天馬・神獣。身体は白馬, 頭は冠をかぶった人間の女性で, 背中に翼, 尾に孔雀のような羽根飾りがついている》

□ **burial** 名埋葬

□ **burn** 動燃える, 燃やす

□ **bury** 動埋葬する, 埋める

□ **business** 名①職業, 仕事 ②商売 ③用事 ④出来事, やっかいなこと **take someone on a business trip** (人) を出張に連れて行く

□ **businessman** 名ビジネスマン, 実業家

□ **busy** 形①忙しい ②にぎやかな, 交通が激しい

□ **but** 接①でも, しかし ②〜を除いて **not 〜 but …** 〜ではなくて… 前〜を除いて, 〜のほかは 副ただ, のみ, ほんの

□ **buy** 動買う, 獲得する

□ **by** 前①《位置》〜のそばに [で] ②《手段・方法・行為者・基準》〜によって, 〜で ③《期限》〜までには ④《通過・経由》〜を経由して, 〜を通って **by now** 今のところ, 今ごろまでには **by oneself** 一人で, 自分だけで, 独力で **by the time** 〜する時までに 副そばに, 通り過ぎて **go by** ①(時が) 過ぎる, 経過する ②〜のそばを通る ③〜に基づいて [よって] 行う **pass by** 〜のそばを通る [通り過ぎる] **walk by** 通りかかる

C

□ **Caesar** 名カエサル《ローマ皇帝の称号》

□ **cake** 名菓子, ケーキ **rice cake** 餅

□ **calendar** 名カレンダー, 暦

□ **call** 動 ①呼ぶ, 叫ぶ ②電話をかける ③立ち寄る **call out** 叫ぶ, 呼び出す, 声を掛ける **call together** 呼び集める, 集合する 名 ①呼び声, 叫び ②電話 (をかけること) ③短い訪問

□ **calling** 動 call (呼ぶ) の現在分詞

□ **calm** 形 穏やかな, 落ち着いた 動 静まる, 静める

□ **calmly** 副 落ち着いて, 静かに

□ **came** 動 come (来る) の過去

□ **camel** 名 ラクダ

□ **can** 助 ①~できる ②~してもよい ③~でありうる ④《否定文で》~のはずがない **can't help** 避けられない, ~せずにはいられない

□ **Capernaum** 名 カファルナウム《ガリラヤ湖の北西岸にある町》

□ **caravan** 名 キャラバン, 隊商, 幌馬車, 移動住宅

□ **care** 名 ①心配, 注意 ②世話, 介護 **take care of** ~の世話をする, ~の面倒を見る, ~を管理する 動 ①《通例否定文・疑問文で》気にする, 心配する ②世話をする **care about** ~を気に掛ける

□ **careful** 形 注意深い, 慎重な

□ **carefully** 副 注意深く, 丹念に

□ **carry** 動 ①運ぶ, 連れていく, 持ち歩く ②伝わる, 伝える **be carried away** 我を忘れる, うっとりする

□ **caste system** カースト制

□ **cause** 名 原因, 理由, 動機

□ **cave** 名 洞穴, 洞窟

□ **celebrate** 動 ①祝う, 祝福する ②祝典を開く

□ **celebration** 名 ①祝賀 ②祝典, 儀式

□ **center** 名 ①中心, 中央 ②中心地 [人物]

□ **chakravarti** 名 チャクラバルティ, 転輪聖王 (てんりんじょうおう)《古代インドの思想における理想的な王を指す概念》

□ **challenge** 動 挑む, 試す

□ **challenger** 名 挑戦者, チャレンジャー

□ **chamber** 名 部屋, 室

□ **chance** 名 ①偶然, 運 ②好機 ③見込み

□ **change** 動 変わる, 変える 名 変化, 変更

□ **Channa** 名 チャンナ, 車匿 (しゃのく)《釈迦が出家する際に, 白馬カンタカを牽引した馬丁》

□ **chant** 名 詠唱

□ **chaplain** 名 司祭, 牧師

□ **character** 名 ①特性, 個性 ②(小説・劇などの) 登場人物 ③文字, 記号 ④品性, 人格

□ **chariot** 名 (古代の) 一人乗り二輪馬車

□ **charming** 形 魅力的な, チャーミングな

□ **cheer** 動 かっさいを送る

□ **chief** 名 頭, 長, 親分 形 最高位の, 第一の, 主要な

□ **child** 名 子ども

□ **children** 名 child (子ども) の複数

□ **choice** 名 選択 (の範囲・自由)

□ **choose** 動 選ぶ, (~に) 決める

□ **chose** 動 choose (選ぶ) の過去

□ **chosen** 動 choose (選ぶ) の過去分詞

□ **Christian** 名 キリスト教徒, クリスチャン 形 キリスト (教) の

□ **Chunda** 名 チュンダ, 純陀 (じゅんだ, ちゅんだ)《鍛冶屋・工巧師の子。釈迦の最期の布施者》

□ **circle** 名 ①円, 円周, 輪 ②循環, 軌道

□ **city** 名 ①都市, 都会 ②《the –》(全) 市民

□ **clan** 名 ①氏族 ②一家, 一門

□ **clean** 形 ①きれいな, 清潔な ②正

当な 動掃除する, よごれを落とす

□ **cleansing** 名浄罪

□ **clear** 形 ①はっきりした, 明白な ②澄んだ ③(よく)晴れた

□ **clearly** 副 ①明らかに, はっきりと ②《返答に用いて》そのとおり

□ **clever** 形 ①頭のよい, 利口な ②器用な, 上手な

□ **cliff** 名断崖, 絶壁

□ **climb** 動登る, 徐々に上がる **climb on** ～の上によじ登る

□ **clinging** 形粘着性の **clinging substance** ここでは固まった血のこと

□ **cloak** 名マント, 袖なし外とう

□ **close** 形 ①近い ②親しい ③狭い **be close to** ～に近い 動 ①閉まる, 閉める ②終える, 閉店する

□ **closely** 副 ①密接に ②念入りに, 詳しく ③ぴったりと

□ **closeness** 名 (距離の)近さ, (関係の)親密さ

□ **cloth** 名布(地), テーブルクロス, ふきん

□ **clothes** 名衣服, 身につけるもの

□ **clothing** 名衣類, 衣料品

□ **cloud** 名雲

□ **cobra** 名コブラ

□ **coin** 名硬貨, コイン

□ **cold** 形 ①寒い, 冷たい ②冷淡な, 冷静な 名 ①寒さ, 冷たさ ②風邪

□ **color** 名色, 色彩

□ **colt** 名 (雄の)子馬

□ **come** 動 ①来る, 行く, 現れる ②(出来事が)起こる, 生じる ③～になる ④comeの過去分詞 **come and** ～しに行く **come back** 戻る **come for** ～の目的で来る, ～を取りに来る **come in** 中にはいる, やってくる **come into** ～に入ってくる **come out** 出てくる, 出掛ける, 姿を現す, 発行される **come out of** ～から出て

くる, ～をうまく乗り越える **come over to** ～にやって来る **come through** 通り抜ける, 成功する, 期待に沿う **come true** 実現する **come up** 近づいてくる, 浮上する, 水面へ上ってくる

□ **comfort** 名 ①快適さ, 満足 ②慰め ③安楽

□ **coming** 動 come (来る)の現在分詞 名到来, 来ること

□ **command** 動命令する, 指揮する

□ **commandment** 名命令, 戒律

□ **common** 形 ①共通の, 共同の ②普通の, 平凡な ③一般の, 公共の

□ **community** 名 ①団体, 共同社会, 地域社会 ②《the –》社会(一般), 世間 ③共有, 共同責任

□ **compare** 動 ①比較する, 対照する ②たとえる **be compared with** ～と比較して, ～に比べれば

□ **compassion** 名思いやり, 深い同情

□ **complete** 動完成させる

□ **completely** 副完全に, すっかり

□ **concentrate** 動一点に集める[集まる], 集中させる[する]

□ **concentration** 名集中, 集中力, 集合 **right concentration** 正定(しょうじょう)《正しい精神統一》

□ **conduct** 名 ①行い, 振る舞い ②指導, 指揮 **right conduct** 正業(しょうごう)《正しい行い》

□ **confidence** 名自信, 確信, 信頼, 信用度

□ **confusion** 名混乱(状態)

□ **connect** 動つながる, つなぐ, 関係づける

□ **consciousness** 名意識, 自覚, 気づいていること

□ **continue** 動続く, 続ける, (中断後)再開する, (ある方向に)移動していく

□ **control** 動 ①管理[支配]する ②

抑制する, コントロールする 图①管理, 支配(力) ②抑制 **in control** ～を支配して, ～を掌握している 〜を制御[管理]する, 支配する **take control of** 〜を制御[管理]する, 支配する

□ **convince** 動 納得させる, 確信させる

□ **cooperate** 動 協力する, 一致団結する

□ **couch** 图 長いす

□ **could** 助①can (～できる) の過去②《控え目な推量・可能性・願望などを表す》**How could 〜?** 何だって〜なんてことがありえようか〜

□ **council** 图 会議, 評議会, 議会

□ **country** 图 国

□ **couple** 图 夫婦, 一組

□ **courage** 图 勇気, 度胸

□ **course** 熟 **of course** もちろん, 当然

□ **court** 图①法廷, 裁判所 ②宮廷, 宮殿

□ **cousin** 图 いとこ

□ **cover** 動 覆う, 包む, 隠す

□ **cow** 图 雌牛, 乳牛

□ **create** 動 創造する, 生み出す, 引き起こす

□ **crime** 图①(法律上の) 罪, 犯罪 ②悪事, よくない行為

□ **crop** 图 作物, 収穫

□ **cross** 動 横切る, 渡る 图 十字架

□ **crowd** 图 群集, 雑踏, 多数, 聴衆

□ **crucify** 動 (十字架に〜を) 張り付けにする

□ **cry** 動 泣く, 叫ぶ, 大声を出す, 嘆く **cry out** 叫ぶ

□ **crying** 形 泣き叫ぶ

□ **culture** 图①文化 ②教養

□ **cup** 图 カップ, 茶わん

□ **curly** 形 巻き毛の

□ **curtain** 图 カーテン

□ **cushion** 图 クッション, 背[座]布団

□ **custom** 图 習慣, 慣例, 風俗

□ **cut** 動 切る, 刈る ②cutの過去, 過去分詞 **cut off** 切断する, 切り離す

D

□ **damage** 動 損害を与える, 損なう

□ **dance** 图 ダンス

□ **danger** 图 危険, 障害, 脅威

□ **dangerous** 形 危険な, 有害な

□ **dare** 動 思い切って[あえて]〜する **How dare you 〜** よくも〜できるね。

□ **darkness** 图 暗さ, 暗やみ

□ **date** 图 日付, 年月日

□ **daughter** 图 娘

□ **day** 图①日中, 昼間 ②日, 期日 ③《-s》時代, 生涯 **each day** 毎日, 日ごとに **every day** 毎日 **one day** (過去の) ある日, (未来の) いつか

□ **day-to-day** 形 毎日の, 日常的な

□ **dead** 形①死んでいる, 活気のない, 枯れた ②まったくの 图《the -》死者たち, 故人

□ **dear** 形 いとしい, 親愛なる, 大事な

□ **death** 图①死, 死ぬこと ②《the -》終えん, 消滅 **to death** 死ぬまで, 死ぬほど

□ **decide** 動 決定[決意]する, (〜しようとと) 決める, 判決を下す

□ **decision** 图①決定, 決心 ②判決

□ **deep** 形 深い

□ **deeply** 副 深く, 非常に

□ **defeat** 图 敗北

□ **defend** 動 防ぐ, 守る, 弁護する

□ **deliver** 動 配達する, 伝える

□ **depend** 動《- on [upon] 〜》①〜を頼る, 〜をあてにする ②〜による

A
B
C
D
E
F
G
H
I
J
K
L
M
N
O
P
Q
R
S
T
U
V
W
X
Y
Z

□ **describe** 動 (言葉で) 描写する, 特色を述べる, 説明する

□ **desert** 名 砂漠

□ **deserve** 動 (〜を) 受けるに足る, 値する, (〜して) 当然である

□ **desperate** 形 ①絶望的な, 見込みのない ②ほしくてたまらない, 必死の

□ **destroy** 動 破壊する, 絶滅させる, 無効にする

□ **deva** 名 デーヴァ (ヒンドゥー教・仏教の) 神

□ **Devadatta** 名 デーヴァダッタ, 提婆達多 (だいばだった)《釈迦のいとこで出家前の釈迦の競争相手。釈迦の出家後に弟子となったが, のちに離反した》

□ **dharma** 名 ダルマ, 法《インドの宗教・思想上の重要概念で, 仏教では, 仏陀の悟った絶対かつ普遍の真理のこと》

□ **dharmic** 形 宗教的《dharma (仏教における法) の形容詞形》

□ **did** 動 do (〜をする) の過去 助 do の過去

□ **die** 動 死ぬ, 消滅する

□ **difference** 名 違い, 相違, 差

□ **different** 形 異なった, 違った, 別の, さまざまな **be different from** 〜と違う

□ **difficult** 形 困難な, むずかしい, 扱いにくい

□ **dig** 動 掘る

□ **dinner** 名 ディナー, 夕食

□ **dirt** 名 ①汚れ, 泥, ごみ ②土

□ **dirty** 形 ①汚い, 汚れた ②卑劣な, 不正な

□ **disappear** 動 見えなくなる, 姿を消す, なくなる

□ **disciple** 名 弟子, 門人

□ **discover** 動 発見する, 気づく

□ **disgust** 名 不快感, 嫌悪

□ **dislike** 動 嫌う

□ **disown** 動 (〜と) 縁を切る

□ **disrespect** 名 尊敬を欠くこと, 軽視, 無礼

□ **distance** 名 距離, 隔たり, 遠方

□ **disturb** 動 かき乱す, 妨げる

□ **divide** 動 分かれる, 分ける, 割れる, 割る **be divided into** 分けられる **divide into** 〜に分かれる

□ **divine** 形 神聖な, 神の **divine being** 神, 天主

□ **do** 助 ①《ほかの動詞とともに用いて現在形の否定文・疑問文をつくる》②《同じ動詞を繰り返す代わりに用いる》③《動詞を強調するのに用いる》動 〜をする

□ **doctor** 名 医者

□ **does** 動 do (〜をする) の3人称単数現在 助 do の3人称単数現在

□ **done** 動 do (〜をする) の過去分詞

□ **door** 名 ①ドア, 戸 ②一軒, 一戸

□ **doubt** 名 ①疑い, 不確かなこと ②未解決点, 困難

□ **dove** 名 ハト (鳩)

□ **down** 副 ①下へ, 降りて, 低くなって ②倒れて 前 〜の下方へ, 〜を下って **fall down** 落ちる, 転ぶ **go down** 下に降りる **let down** 期待を裏切る, 失望させる **push down** 押し倒す **put down** 下に置く, 下ろす

□ **dream** 名 夢, 幻想

□ **dress** 動 ①服を着る [着せる] ②飾る

□ **drink** 名 飲み物

□ **drive** 動 車で行く **drive home** 車で家に帰る

□ **driver** 名 ①運転手 ②(馬車の) 御者

□ **drove** 動 drive (車で行く) の過去

□ **dry** 形 ①乾燥した ②辛口の 動 乾燥する [させる], 干す

□ **dung** 名 (牛馬の) 糞

□ **during** 前 ～の間（ずっと）

□ **dust** 名 ちり，ほこり

□ **dusty** 形 ほこりだらけの

□ **duty** 名 ①義務（感），責任 ②職務，任務，関税

□ **dying** 動 die（死ぬ）の現在分詞 形 死にかかっている，消えそうな

E

□ **each** 形 それぞれの，各自の **each day** 毎日，日ごとに **each one** 各自 **each other** お互いに 代 それぞれ，各自 副 それぞれに

□ **early** 形 （時間や時期が）早い 副 早く，早めに

□ **earn** 動 儲ける，稼ぐ

□ **earth** 名 ①《the –》地球 ②大地，陸地，土 ③この世 **on earth** 地球上で，この世で

□ **earthly** 形 地上の，現世の

□ **easily** 副 ①容易に，たやすく，苦もなく ②気楽に

□ **east** 名 《the –》東，東部，東方

□ **easy** 形 ①やさしい，簡単な ②気楽な，くつろいだ

□ **eat** 動 食べる，食事する

□ **eaten** 動 eat（食べる）の過去分詞

□ **edge** 名 ①刃 ②端，縁

□ **educated** 形 教養のある，教育を受けた

□ **effect** 名 影響，効果，結果

□ **effort** 名 努力（の成果）

□ **eight** 名 8（の数字），8人［個］ 形 8の，8人［個］の

□ **eighteen-year-old** 形 18歳の

□ **eightfold** 形 8倍の，八重の

□ **eightfold path** 八正道（はっしょうどう）《仏教において涅槃に至るための8つの実践徳目である正見，正思惟，正語，正業，正命，正精進，正念，正定のこと》

□ **eighth** 名 第8番目（の人［物］），8日 形 第8番目の

□ **either** 形 ①（2つのうち）どちらかの ②どちらでも 代 どちらも，どちらでも 副 ①どちらか ②《否定文で》～もまた（…ない） 接《- ～ or …》～かまたは…か

□ **elder** 形 年上の，年長の

□ **elephant** 名 象

□ **eleven** 名 ①11（の数字），11人［個］ ②11人のチーム，イレブン 形 11の，11人［個］の

□ **Elijah** 名 エリヤ《古代イスラエル民族の預言》

□ **eliminate** 動 削除［排除・除去］する，撤廃する

□ **Elizabeth** 名 エリサベト《洗礼者ヨハネの母》

□ **else** 副 ①そのほかに［の］，代わりに ②さもないと **anything else** ほかの何か **no one else** 他の誰一人として～しない

□ **embarrassed** 形 恥ずかしい，当惑して

□ **emperor** 名 皇帝，天皇

□ **end** 名 ①終わり，終末，死 ②果て，末，端 ③目的 **in the end** とうとう，結局，ついに **put an end to** ～に終止符を打つ，～を終わらせる，～に決着をつける 動 終わる，終える

□ **endeavor** 名 努力 **right endeavor** 正精進（しょうしょうじん）《正しい努力，修養》

□ **endure** 動 ①我慢する，耐え忍ぶ ②持ちこたえる

□ **enemy** 名 敵

□ **energy** 名 ①力，勢い ②元気，精力，エネルギー

□ **enjoy** 動 楽しむ，享受する

□ **enlightened** 形 悟りに達した，悟りを開いた

□ **enlightenment** 名 啓発，啓蒙，

143

A
B
C
D
E
F
G
H
I
J
K
L
M
N
O
P
Q
R
S
T
U
V
W
X
Y
Z

教化

- [ ] **enough** 形十分な，(〜するに)足る **enough to do** 〜するのに十分な 代十分(な量・数)，たくさん 副(〜できる)だけ，十分に，まったく

- [ ] **enter** 動①入る，入会[入学]する[させる] ②記入する ③(考えなどが)(心・頭に)浮かぶ

- [ ] **entire** 形全体の，完全な，まったくの

- [ ] **entrance** 名①入り口，入場 ②開始

- [ ] **environment** 名①環境 ②周囲(の状況)，情勢

- [ ] **equal** 形等しい，均等な，平等な 名同等のもの[人]

- [ ] **escape** 動逃げる，免れる，もれる 名逃亡，脱出，もれ

- [ ] **especially** 副特別に，とりわけ

- [ ] **even** 副《強意》〜でさえも，〜ですら，いっそう，なおさら **even if** たとえ〜でも **even though** 〜であるけれども，〜にもかかわらず

- [ ] **evening** 名夕方，晩

- [ ] **ever** 副①今までに，これまで，かつて，いつまでも ②《強意》いったい

- [ ] **every** 形①どの〜も，すべての，あらゆる ②毎〜，〜ごとの **every day** 毎日

- [ ] **everybody** 代誰でも，皆

- [ ] **everyone** 代誰でも，皆

- [ ] **everything** 代すべてのこと[もの]，何でも，何もかも

- [ ] **evil** 形①邪悪な ②有害な，不吉な

- [ ] **exactly** 副①正確に，厳密に，ちょうど ②まったくそのとおり

- [ ] **example** 名例，見本，模範

- [ ] **excellent** 形優れた，優秀な

- [ ] **except** 前〜を除いて，〜のほかは **except for** 〜を除いて，〜がなければ

- [ ] **excited** 形興奮した，わくわくし

- [ ] **excitement** 名興奮(すること)

- [ ] **exclaim** 動①(喜び・驚きなどで)声をあげる ②声高に激しく言う

- [ ] **exist** 動存在する，生存する，ある，いる

- [ ] **expect** 動予期[予測]する，(当然のこととして)期待する

- [ ] **expensive** 形高価な，ぜいたくな

- [ ] **experience** 動経験[体験]する

- [ ] **experienced** 形経験のある，経験を積んだ

- [ ] **explain** 動説明する，明らかにする，釈明[弁明]する

- [ ] **eye** 名目

F

- [ ] **face** 名顔

- [ ] **fact** 名事実，真相 **in fact** つまり，実は，要するに

- [ ] **fail** 動①失敗する，落第する[させる] ②《-to〜》〜し損なう，〜できない ③失望させる

- [ ] **faint** 動気絶する

- [ ] **fair** 形正しい，公平[正当]な

- [ ] **fairly** 副公平に

- [ ] **faith** 名①信念，信仰 ②信頼，信用

- [ ] **faithfully** 副忠実に，正確に

- [ ] **fall** 動①落ちる，倒れる ②(ある状態に)急に陥る **fall asleep** 眠り込む，寝入る **fall down** 落ちる，転ぶ **fall to the ground** 転ぶ

- [ ] **fallen** 動 fall (落ちる) の過去分詞 形落ちた，倒れた

- [ ] **fame** 名評判，名声

- [ ] **familiar** 形①親しい，親密な ②普通の，いつもの，おなじみの

- [ ] **family** 名家族，家庭，一門，家柄

- [ ] **famous** 形有名な，名高い

□ **far** 副 ①遠くに, はるかに, 離れて ②《比較級を強めて》ずっと, はるかに 形遠い, 向こうの **far from** 〜から遠い, 〜どころか

□ **fast** 副速く, 急いで

□ **father** 名 ①父親 ②神父, 司祭

□ **Fatima** 名 ①ファーティマ (・ビント・アサド)《ムハンマドの叔母》②ファーティマ《ムハンマドの娘》

□ **favor** 動好意を示す, 賛成する

□ **favorite** 名お気に入り (の人[物]) 形お気に入りの, ひいきの

□ **fear** 名 ①恐れ ②心配, 不安 動 ①恐れる ②心配する

□ **fed** 動feed (食物を与える) の過去, 過去分詞

□ **feed** 動食物を与える

□ **feel** 動感じる, (〜と) 思う **feel better** 気分がよくなる

□ **feeling** 動feel (感じる) の現在分詞 名 ①感じ, 気持ち ②触感, 知覚 ③同情, 思いやり, 感受性 形感じる, 感じやすい, 情け深い

□ **feet** 名foot (足) の複数 **get to one's feet** 立ち上がる **jump to one's feet** 突然[いきなり]立ち上がる **jump to one's feet** 飛び起きる

□ **fell** 動fall (落ちる) の過去

□ **fellow** 名仲間, 同僚

□ **felt** 動feel (感じる) の過去, 過去分詞

□ **fever** 名 ①熱 ②熱病

□ **few** 形 ①ほとんどない, 少数の (〜しかない) ②《a −》少数の, 少しはある

□ **field** 名野原, 田畑, 広がり

□ **fierce** 形どう猛な, 荒々しい, すさまじい, 猛烈な

□ **fifth** 名第5番目 (の人[物]), 5日 形第5番目の

□ **fiftieth** 形 ①《the −》50番目の ②50分の1の 名 ①《the −》50番目 ②50分の1

□ **fight** 動 (〜と) 戦う, 争う **fight back** 反撃に転じる, 応戦する 名戦い, 争い

□ **fighter** 名戦士

□ **fighting** 名戦闘

□ **figure** 名人[物]の姿, 形

□ **fill** 動 ①満ちる, 満たす ②《be -ed with 〜》〜でいっぱいである

□ **final** 形最後の, 決定的な

□ **finally** 副最後に, ついに, 結局

□ **find** 動 ①見つける ②(〜と) わかる, 気づく, 〜と考える ③得る **find out** 見つけ出す, 気がつく, 知る, 調べる, 解明する

□ **fine** 形 ①元気な ②美しい, りっぱな, 申し分ない, 結構な ③晴れた ④細かい, 微妙な

□ **finger** 名 (手の) 指

□ **finish** 動終わる, 終える

□ **fire** 名火, 炎, 火事 **set on fire** 火をつける

□ **first** 名最初, 第一 (の人・物) **at first** 最初は, 初めのうちは 形 ①第一の, 最初の ②最も重要な 副第一に, 最初に

□ **fisher** 名漁師

□ **fisherman** 名漁師, (趣味の) 釣り人

□ **fishermen** 名fisherman (漁師) の複数形

□ **fishers of people** 人間の漁をする (人を集める) 漁師

□ **five** 名5 (の数字), 5人[個] 形5の, 5人[個] の

□ **flag** 名旗

□ **flame** 名炎

□ **flesh** 名肉

□ **flood** 名洪水

□ **floor** 名床

□ **flow** 名流出

□ **flower** 名花

- ☐ **fly** 動 飛ぶ, 飛ばす

- ☐ **focus** ①焦点を合わせる ②(関心・注意を)集中させる

- ☐ **follow** 動 ①ついていく, あとをたどる ②(〜の)結果として起こる ③(忠告などに)従う ④理解できる

- ☐ **follower** 名 信奉者, 追随者

- ☐ **following** 動 follow (ついていく)の現在分詞 形《the −》次の, 次に続く

- ☐ **food** 名 食物, えさ

- ☐ **foot** 名 ①足 ②(山などの)ふもと, (物の)最下部, すそ **get to one's feet** 立ち上がる **jump to one's feet** 突然[いきなり]立ち上がる **jump to one's feet** 飛び起きる **at the foot of** 〜のすそ[下部]に

- ☐ **for** 前 ①《目的・原因・対象》〜にとって, 〜のために[の], 〜に対して ②《期間》〜間 ③《代理》〜の代わりに ④《方向》〜へ(向かって) **for oneself** 独力で, 自分のために **for the rest of life** 死ぬまで **for years** 何年も **for 〜 years** 〜年間, 〜年にわたって 接 というわけは〜, なぜなら〜, だから

- ☐ **force** 動 ①強制する, 力ずくで〜する, 余儀なく〜させる ②押しやる, 押し込む

- ☐ **forest** 名 森林

- ☐ **forever** 副 永遠に, 絶えず

- ☐ **forget** 動 忘れる, 置き忘れる

- ☐ **forgive** 動 許す, 免除する

- ☐ **forgiven** 動 forgive (許す)の過去分詞

- ☐ **forgiveness** 名 許す(こと), 寛容

- ☐ **forgot** 動 forget (忘れる)の過去, 過去分詞

- ☐ **form** 名 ①形, 形式 ②書式

- ☐ **former** 形 ①前の, 先の, 以前の ②《the −》(二者のうち)前者の

- ☐ **forsake** 動 (〜を)見捨てる, (〜を)見放す

- ☐ **forsaken** 動 forsake (〜を見捨てる)の過去分詞形

- ☐ **forty** 名 40(の数字), 40人[個] 形 40の, 40人[個]の

- ☐ **forward** 副 前方に

- ☐ **fought** 動 fight (戦う)の過去, 過去分詞

- ☐ **found** 動 find (見つける)の過去, 過去分詞

- ☐ **foundation** 名 基礎, 土台

- ☐ **four** 名 4(の数字), 4人[個] 形 4の, 4人[個]の

- ☐ **four noble truths** 四諦(したい)または四聖諦(ししょうたい)《仏教が説く4種の基本的な真理。苦諦(この現実世界は苦であるという真理), 集諦(じったい。苦の原因は迷妄と執着にあるという真理), 滅諦(迷妄を離れ, 執着を断ち切ることが, 悟りの境界にいたることであるという真理), 道諦(悟りの境界にいたる具体的な実践方法は, 八正道であるという真理)のこと》

- ☐ **fourth** 名 第4番目(の人・物), 4日 形 第4番目の

- ☐ **free** 形 ①自由な, 開放された, 自由に〜できる ②(物が)空いている, 使える ③無料の 動 自由にする, 解放する

- ☐ **freedom** 名 ①自由 ②束縛がないこと

- ☐ **friend** 名 友だち, 仲間

- ☐ **from** 前 ①《出身・出発点・時間・順序・原料》〜から ②《原因・理由》〜がもとで **from then on** それ以来

- ☐ **front** 名 正面, 前 **in front of** 〜の前に, 〜の正面に

- ☐ **fruit** 名 果実, 実

- ☐ **frustrated** 形 挫折した, 失望した

- ☐ **fulfill** 動 (義務・約束を)果たす, (要求・条件を)満たす

- ☐ **full** 形 満ちた, いっぱいの

- ☐ **fully** 副 十分に, 完全に, まるまる

146

□ **fun** 图 楽しみ, 冗談, おもしろいこと　**make fun of** ～を物笑いの種にする, からかう

□ **future** 图 未来, 将来

G

□ **Gabriel** 图 ジブリール（ガブリエル）《ムハンマドに神の言葉である『クルアーン』を伝えた大天使》

□ **gain** 動 ①得る, 増す ②進歩する, 進む

□ **Galilee** 图 ガリラヤ《ヨルダン川の西側で, 主にイスラエル北部に当たる地域》**Sea of Galilee** ガリラヤ湖《イスラエル北東部。ヨルダン川につながる湖》

□ **garden** 图 庭, 庭園

□ **garland** 图 花飾り, 花冠 **garland of fingers** アングリマーラ, 指鬘（しまん）《殺した人の指を切り取って作った鬘（かずら, 首飾り）》

□ **gate** 图 ①門, 扉, 入り口 ②（空港・駅などの）ゲート

□ **gather** 動 ①集まる, 集める ②生じる, 増す ③推測する

□ **gave** 動 give（与える）の過去

□ **Gaya** 图 ガヤー, ブッダガヤ《インド東部ビハール州, ガヤー県にある仏教の聖地》

□ **generosity** 图 ①寛大, 気前のよさ ②豊富さ

□ **generous** 形 ①寛大な, 気前のよい ②豊富な

□ **Gennesaret** 图 ゲネサレト《ガリラヤ湖の西側にある平原地帯の名》

□ **gently** 副 親切に, 上品に, そっと, 優しく

□ **get** 動 ①得る, 手に入れる ②（ある状態に）なる, いたる ③わかる, 理解する ④～させる, ～を（…の状態に）する ⑤（ある場所に）達する, 着く **get away** 逃げる, 逃亡する, 離れる

get in 中に入る, 乗り込む **get into trouble** 面倒を起こす, 困った事になる, トラブルに巻き込まれる **get into trouble with** ～とトラブルを起こす **get near** 接近する **get off**（～から）降りる ①外に出る, 出て行く, 逃げ出す ②取り出す, 抜き出す **get ready** 用意［支度］をする **get to** （事）を始める, ～に達する［到着する］**get to one's feet** 立ち上がる **get up** 起き上がる, 立ち上がる

□ **Gethsemane** 图 ゲッセマネ《エルサレムのオリーブ山の北西麓にあった地名》

□ **gift** 图 贈り物

□ **girl** 图 女の子, 少女

□ **give** 動 ①与える, 贈る ②伝える, 述べる ③（～を）する **give away** ①ただで与える, 贈る, 譲歩する, 手放す ②（素性・正体を）暴露する, 馬脚を現す **give up** あきらめる, やめる, 引き渡す

□ **given** 動 give（与える）の過去分詞

□ **gloat** 動 満足げに眺める, ほくそ笑む

□ **glow** 動 （火が）白熱して輝く 图 ①白熱, 輝き ②ほてり, 熱情

□ **go** 動 ①行く, 出かける ②動く ③進む, 経過する, いたる ④（ある状態に）なる **be going to** ～するつもりである **go across** 横断する, 渡る **go ahead** 先に行く, 《許可を表す》どうぞ **go around** 動き回る, あちらこちらに行く, 回り道をする, （障害）を回避する **go away** 立ち去る **go back to** ～に帰る［戻る］, ～に遡る, （中断していた作業に）再び取り掛かる **go by** ①（時が）過ぎる, 経過する ②～のそばを通る ③～に基づいて［よって］行う **go down** 下に降りる **go home** 帰宅する **go into** ～に入る, （仕事）に就く **go off** ①出かける, 去る, 出発する ②始める, 突然～しだす ③（電気が）消える **go on** 続く, 続ける, 進み続ける, 起こる, 発生する **go out** 外出する, 外へ出る **go through** 通り抜ける, 一つずつ順番

に検討する **go to hell** 地獄に落ちる, くたばる **go to sleep** 寝る **go up** ① ～に上がる, 登る ②～に近づく, 出かける ③(建物などが) 建つ, 立つ **go up to** ～まで行く, 近づく **go with** ～と一緒に行く, ～と調和する, ～にとても似合う **let go of** ～から手を離す

- [ ] **god** 名 神 **pray to God for** ～を神に祈る
- [ ] **gold** 名 金, 金貨, 金製品, 金色 形 金の, 金製の, 金色の
- [ ] **golden** 形 ①金色の ②金製の ③貴重な
- [ ] **Golgotha** 名 ゴルゴタ《エルサレム付近の丘》
- [ ] **gone** 動 go (行く) の過去分詞 形 去った, 使い果たした, 死んだ
- [ ] **good** 形 ①よい, 上手な, 優れた, 美しい ②(数量・程度が) かなりの, 相当な **be good at** ～が得意だ 名 《-s》財産, 品, 物質
- [ ] **good-bye** 名 別れのあいさつ
- [ ] **good-looking** 形 顔形の整った, 容姿端麗な
- [ ] **goodbye** 名 別れのあいさつ
- [ ] **goodness** 名 ①善良さ, よいところ ②優秀
- [ ] **goods** 名 ①商品, 品物 ②財産, 所有物
- [ ] **got** 動 get (得る) の過去, 過去分詞
- [ ] **gotten** 動 get (得る) の過去分詞
- [ ] **governor** 名 知事
- [ ] **grab** 動 ふいにつかむ
- [ ] **grandfather** 名 祖父
- [ ] **grandson** 名 孫息子, 男の孫
- [ ] **great** 形 ①大きい, 広大な, (量や程度が) たいへんな ②偉大な, 優れた ③すばらしい, おもしろい
- [ ] **greatly** 副 大いに
- [ ] **greed** 名 どん欲, 欲張り
- [ ] **green** 形 緑色の

- [ ] **greet** 動 ①あいさつする ②(喜んで) 迎える
- [ ] **grew** 動 grow (成長する) の過去
- [ ] **grey** 形 ①灰色の ②白髪の
- [ ] **ground** 名 地面, 土, 土地 **fall to the ground** 転ぶ **on the ground** 地面に
- [ ] **group** 名 集団, 群
- [ ] **grow** 動 ①成長する, 育つ, 育てる ②増大する, 大きくなる, (次第に～) になる **grow into** 成長して～になる **grow up** 成長する, 大人になる
- [ ] **growing** 動 grow ((次第に～に) なる) の現在分詞
- [ ] **guard** 名 ①警戒, 見張り ②番人
- [ ] **guide** 名 ①ガイド, 手引き, 入門書 ②案内人

H

- [ ] **had** 動 have (持つ) の過去, 過去分詞 助 have の過去《過去完了の文をつくる》
- [ ] **hair** 名 髪, 毛
- [ ] **hajj** 名 ハッジ《マッカへの巡礼》
- [ ] **half** 半分の, 不完全な
- [ ] **Halima** ハリーマ (・サアディーヤ) 《ムハンマドの養母》
- [ ] **Hamza** ハムザ (・ブン・アブド・アル＝ムッタリブ)《ムハンマドの叔父》
- [ ] **hand** 名 手 動 手渡す
- [ ] **hang** 動 かかる, かける, つるす, ぶら下がる
- [ ] **happen** 動 ①(出来事が) 起こる, 生じる ②偶然 [たまたま] ～する **happen to** たまたま～する, 偶然～する
- [ ] **happily** 副 幸福に, 楽しく, うまく, 幸いにも
- [ ] **happiness** 名 幸せ, 喜び

□ **happy** 形 幸せな, うれしい, 幸運な, 満足して **be happy to do** 〜してうれしい, 喜んで〜する

□ **hard** 形 ①堅い ②激しい, むずかしい ③熱心な, 勤勉な ④無情な, 耐えがたい, 厳しい, きつい **a hard time** つらい時期 **hard to** 〜し難い 副 ①一生懸命に ②激しく ③堅く

□ **harm** 動 傷つける, 損なう

□ **harmful** 形 害を及ぼす, 有害な

□ **harmless** 形 無害の, 安全な

□ **has** 動 have (持つ)の3人称単数現在 助 have の3人称単数現在《現在完了の文をつくる》

□ **hate** 動 嫌う, 憎む, (〜するのを)いやがる 名 憎しみ

□ **hatred** 名 憎しみ, 毛嫌い

□ **have** 動 ①持つ, 持っている, 抱く ②(〜が)ある, いる ③食べる, 飲む ④経験する, (病気に)かかる ⑤催す, 開く ⑥(人に)〜させる **have to** 〜しなければならない **don't have to** 〜する必要はない **have a baby boy** 男の子を産む **have power over** 〜を思いのままに操る力を持っている 助《〈have＋過去分詞〉の形で現在完了の文をつくる》〜した, 〜したことがある, ずっと〜している **should have done** 〜すべきだった (のにしなかった)《仮定法》 **would have … if** 〜 もし〜だったとしたら…しただろう

□ **he** 代 彼は [が]

□ **head** 名 ①頭 ②先頭 ③長, 指導者 **head of** 〜の長

□ **heal** 動 いえる, いやす, 治る, 治す

□ **healing** 動 heal (いえる)の現在分詞 形 治療の, 病気を治す, いやす

□ **hear** 動 聞く, 聞こえる **hear about** 〜について聞く **hear of** 〜について聞く

□ **heard** 動 hear (聞く)の過去, 過去分詞

□ **heart** 名 ①心臓, 胸 ②心, 感情, ハート ③中心, 本質 **with all one's heart** 心から

□ **heartfelt** 形 心からの, 心のある

□ **heaven** 名 天国

□ **held** 動 hold (つかむ)の過去, 過去分詞

□ **hell** 名 地獄, 地獄のようなところ[状態] **go to hell** 地獄に落ちる, くたばる

□ **help** 動 ①助ける, 手伝う ②給仕する **can't help** 避けられない, 〜せずにはいられない 名 助け, 手伝い

□ **her** 代 ①彼女を [に] ②彼女の

□ **herb** 名 薬草, 香草, ハーブ

□ **here** 副 ①ここに[で] ②《- is [are] 〜》ここに〜がある ③さあ, そら 名 ここ **here and now** 今この場で

□ **hero** 名 英雄, ヒーロー

□ **Herod, King** ヘロデ大王《共和政ローマ末期からローマ帝国初期にユダヤ王国を統治した王》

□ **herself** 代 彼女自身

□ **hey** 間 ①《呼びかけ・注意を促して》おい, ちょっと ②へえ, おや, まあ

□ **hide** 動 隠れる, 隠す, 隠れて見えない, 秘密にする

□ **high** 形 ①高い ②気高い, 高価な **High God** 高神 副 ①高く ②ぜいたくに

□ **Hijra** 名 ヒジュラ, 聖遷《622年に, ムハンマドとムスリムがマッカからヤスリブ(マディーナ)に移住したこと》

□ **hill** 名 丘, 塚

□ **him** 代 彼を [に]

□ **Himalaya** 名 ヒマラヤ山脈

□ **himself** 代 彼自身

□ **Hira** 名 ヒラーの洞窟《マッカの郊外にそびえる岩山ヒラー山の頂上の南西側にある洞窟》

□ **his** 代 ①彼の ②彼のもの

□ **hit** 動 ①打つ, なぐる ②ぶつける,

149

A
B
C
D
E
F
G
H
I
J
K
L
M
N
O
P
Q
R
S
T
U
V
W
X
Y
Z

ぶつかる ③命中する ④（天災など
が）襲う, 打撃を与える ⑤hitの過去,
過去分詞

□ **hold** 動①つかむ, 持つ, 抱く ②保
つ, 持ちこたえる ③収納できる, 入
れることができる ④（会などを）開
く **hold a meeting** 会議を開く
hold out 差し出す, （腕を）伸ばす
hold up 〜を持ち上げる 名①つか
むこと, 保有 ②支配［理解］力 **take
hold of** 〜をつかむ, 捕らえる, 制す
る

□ **hole** 名穴

□ **holy** 形聖なる, 神聖な **Holy
Spirit** 聖霊

□ **home** 名①家, 自国, 故郷, 家庭 ②
収容所 **at home** 自宅で, 在宅して
go home 帰宅する 副家に, 自国へ

□ **honest** 形①正直な, 誠実な, 心か
らの ②公正な, 感心な

□ **honey** 名蜂蜜（のように甘いもの）

□ **honor** 名①名誉, 光栄, 信用 ②節
操, 自尊心 **honor of doing** 〜する光
栄［栄誉］

□ **hood** 名フード, ずきん

□ **hope** 名希望, 期待, 見込み **in the
hope of** 〜を望んで［期待して］ 動
望む,（〜であるようにと）思う

□ **horse** 名馬

□ **Hosanna** 間ホサナ「神をたたえ
よ」という呼び掛け語《神を賛美する
叫び［言葉］》.

□ **hot** 形①暑い, 熱い ②できたての,
新しい ③からい, 強烈な, 熱中した
副①熱く ②激しく

□ **hour** 名1時間, 時間

□ **house** 名①家, 家庭 ②（特定の目
的のための）建物, 小屋

□ **how** 副①どうやって, どれくらい,
どんなふうに ②なんて（〜だろう）
③《関係副詞》〜する方法 **How
could** 〜？何だって〜なんてことが
ありえようか **How dare you
〜** よくも〜できるね. **how to** 〜す
る方法 **show 〜 how to …** 〜に…の
やり方を示す

□ **however** 腰けれども, だが

□ **Hudaybiyya** 名フダイビーヤ《マ
ッカ郊外の小村》 **Treaty of
Hudaybiyya** フダイビーヤの和議《ム
ハンマドとマッカのクライシュ族の
間で結ばれた和議》

□ **huge** 形巨大な, ばく大な

□ **human** 形人間の, 人の **human
being** 人, 人間 名人間

□ **humble** 形つつましい, 粗末な

□ **hundred** 名①100（の数字）, 100
人［個］ ②《-s》何百, 多数 **hundreds
of** 何百もの〜 形①100の, 100人［個］
の ②多数の

□ **hungry** 形①空腹の, 飢えた ②渇
望して ③不毛の

□ **hunt** 動狩る, 狩りをする

□ **hurry** 急ぐ, 急がせる, あわてる
hurry off 急いで立ち去る, 急いで出
掛ける

□ **hurt** 動傷つける, 痛む, 害する 形
けがをした

□ **husband** 名夫

□ **hut** 名簡易住居, あばら屋, 山小屋

I

□ **I** 代私は［が］

□ **idea** 名考え, 意見, アイデア, 計画

□ **identify** 動①（本人・同一と）確認
する, 見分ける ②意気投合する

□ **identity** 名①同一であること ②
本人であること ③独自性

□ **idol** 名偶像, 崇拝される人（物）

□ **if** 腰もし〜ならば, たとえ〜でも,
〜かどうか **as if** あたかも〜のよう
に, まるで〜みたいに **even if** たとえ
〜でも **if any** もしあれば, あったと
しても **wonder if** 〜ではないかと思
う **would have … if 〜** もし〜だっ
たとしたら…しただろう

150

□ **ignore** 動無視する, 怠る

□ **ill** 形 ①病気の, 不健康な ②悪い

□ **imagine** 動想像する, 心に思い描く

□ **importance** 名重要性, 大切さ

□ **important** 形重要な, 大切な, 有力な

□ **impossible** 形不可能な, できない, あり[起こり]えない

□ **impress** 動印象づける, 感銘させる

□ **impure** 形不純な

□ **in** 前①《場所・位置・所属》~(の中)に[で・の] ②《時》~(の時)に[の・で], ~後(に), ~の間(に) ③《方法・手段》~で ④~を身につけて, ~を着て ⑤~に関して, ~について ⑥《状態》~の状態で 副~の中へ[に], 内へ[に] **in a way** ある意味では **in answer to** ~に応じて **in control** ~を支配して, ~を掌握している **in fact** つまり, 実は, 要するに **in front of** ~の前に, ~の正面に **in one place** 一ヶ所に **in peace** 平和のうちに, 安心して **in person** (本人)自ら, 自身で **in place of** ~の代わりに **in return** お返しとして **in silence** 黙って, 沈黙のうちに **in the end** とうとう, 結局, ついに **in the hope of** ~を望んで[期待して] **in the middle of** ~の真ん中[中ほど]に **in the world** 世界で **in this way** このようにして

□ **include** 動含む, 勘定に入れる

□ **including** 動 include (含む)の現在分詞 前~を含めて, 込みで

□ **independent** 形独立した, 自立した

□ **India** 名インド《国名》

□ **information** 名情報, 通知, 知識

□ **inheritance** 名 ①相続(財産), 遺産 ②遺伝

□ **inner** 形 ①内部の ②心の中の

□ **innocent** 名無邪気な人, 罪のない人 形無邪気な, 無実の

□ **inside** 名内部, 内側 形内部[内側]にある 副内部[内側]に 前~の内部[内側]に

□ **instead** 副その代わりに **instead of** ~の代わりに, ~をしないで

□ **insult** 動侮辱する, ばかにする

□ **intelligent** 形頭のよい, 聡明な

□ **intention** 名 ①意図, (~する)つもり ②心構え **right intention** 正思惟(しょうしゆい)《正しい思考》

□ **interest** 名興味, 関心 動興味を起こさせる

□ **interested** 形興味を持った, 関心のある

□ **into** 前 ①《動作・運動の方向》~の中へ[に] ②《変化》~に[へ]

□ **invite** 動 ①招待する, 招く ②勧める, 誘う ③~をもたらす

□ **involved** 形 ①巻き込まれている, 関連する ②入り組んだ, 込み入っている

□ **is** 動 be (~である)の3人称単数現在

□ **Islam** 名 ①イスラム教[教徒・文化] ②(神への)服従《アラビア語》

□ **isolated** 形隔離した, 孤立した

□ **issue** 名問題, 論点

□ **it** 代 ①それは[が], それを[に] ②《天候・日時・距離・寒暖などを示す》 **It is ~ for someone to …** (人)が…するのは~だ **So be it.** それならそれでいい。

□ **its** 代それの, あれの

□ **itself** 代それ自体, それ自身

J

□ **Jairus** 名ヤイロ《ガリラヤ湖北岸の町カファルナウムの会堂長》

□ **James** 名ヤコブ《十二使徒の一人》

□ **James bar Alpheus** アルファ

イの子のヤコブ《十二使徒の一人》

- □ **jar** 图 (広口の)瓶, 壺

- □ **jealous** 形 嫉妬して, 嫉妬深い, う らやんで

- □ **Jerusalem** 图 エルサレム《イスラ エルにある都市》

- □ **Jesus** 图 ①イエス・キリスト(前4 頃-30頃)《キリスト教の始祖》**Jesus of Nazareth** ナザレのイエス《人名》 ②イーサー(ナザレのイエス)《イス ラム教における呼称》

- □ **Jeta monastery** 祇園精舎(ぎ おんしょうじゃ)《コーサラ国首都シ ュラーヴァスティー(舎衛城)にあっ た寺院。釈迦の大口支援者であったス ダッタ(アナータピンディカ)によっ て, 釈迦に寄贈された》

- □ **Jew** 图 ユダヤ人[教徒]

- □ **jewel** 图 宝石, 貴重な人[物]

- □ **jeweled** 形 宝石で飾られた

- □ **jewelry** 图 宝石, 宝飾品類

- □ **Jewish** 形 ユダヤ人の, ユダヤ教の **Jewish calendar** ユダヤ暦 **Jewish law** ユダヤ法, ユダヤ教の戒律

- □ **job** 图 仕事, 職, 雇用

- □ **John** 图 ヨハネ《十二使徒の一人》

- □ **John the Baptist** 洗礼者ヨハネ 《預言者》

- □ **join** 動 ①一緒になる, 参加する ② 連結[結合]する, つなぐ

- □ **joint** 图 ①継ぎ目, 継ぎ手 ②関節

- □ **Jordan, River** ヨルダン川《イス ラエルのフラ湖とガリラヤ湖を通っ て死海に注ぐ川》

- □ **Joseph** 图 ヨセフ《マリアの夫, イ エスの養父》

- □ **journey** 图 ①(遠い目的地への) 旅 ②行程

- □ **joy** 图 喜び, 楽しみ

- □ **Judas Iscariot** イスカリオテの ユダ《十二使徒の一人》

- □ **judge** 動 判決を下す, 裁く, 判断す

る, 評価する

- □ **jump** 動 跳ぶ, 跳躍する, 飛び越え る, 飛びかかる **jump to one's feet** 突然[いきなり]立ち上がる **jump to one's feet** 飛び起きる

- □ **jungle** 图 ジャングル

- □ **just** 副 ①まさに, ちょうど, (〜し た)ばかり ②ほんの, 単に, ただ〜だ け ③ちょっと **just as** (ちょうど)で あろうとおり

K

- □ **Kaaba** 图 カアバ神殿《マッカのマ スジド・ハラームにある建造物で, イ スラム教における最高の聖地とみな されている聖殿》

- □ **Kanthaka** 图 カンタカ, 健陟《釈 迦が出家したさい乗っていた白馬》

- □ **Kapilavastu** 图 カピラヴァスト ゥ, カピラ城《インド北方のヒマラヤ 山麓にある, シャーキヤ族の都。釈迦 の出身地》

- □ **karma** 图 カルマ, 業, 宿命, 因縁

- □ **Kasi** 图 カーシー《インドのウッタ ル・プラデーシュ州, ヴァーラーナシ ー県の都市ヴァーラーナシー (Varanasi)の古名》

- □ **keep** 動 ①とっておく, 保つ, 続け る ②(〜を…に)しておく ③飼う, 養う ④経営する ⑤守る **keep someone from** 〜から(人)を阻む

- □ **kept** 動 keep (とっておく)の過去, 過去分詞

- □ **kesadhatu** 仏陀の聖髪, 髪舎利 (はっしゃり)

- □ **Khadija** 图 ハディージャ(・ビン ト・フワイリド)《ムハンマドの最初 の妻》

- □ **Khuza'a** 图 クザア族《イエメン出 身のアラブ人の部族》

- □ **kill** 動 殺す

- □ **kind** 形 親切な, 優しい **be kind to**

~に親切である 图種類 **kind of** ある程度, いくらか, ~のようなもの［人］

□ **kindness** 图親切 (な行為), 優しさ

□ **king** 图王, 国王

□ **king cobra** キング・コブラ

□ **King Herod** ヘロデ大王《共和政ローマ末期からローマ帝国初期にユダヤ王国を統治した王》

□ **kingdom** 图王国 **kingdom of God** 神の王国

□ **Kisa Gautami** キサー・ゴータミー《釈迦に導かれ, 子どもを亡くした苦しみから救われた女性》

□ **kiss** 图キス 動キスする

□ **knew** 動know (知っている) の過去

□ **know** 動①知っている, 知る, (~が) わかる, 理解している ②知り合いである

□ **knowledge** 图知識, 理解, 学問

□ **known** 動know (知っている) の過去分詞 形知られた **be known as** ~として知られている

□ **Koliya** 图コーリヤ族《摩耶夫人の出身部族》

□ **Kondanna** 图コンダンニャ, 阿若・憍陳如 (あにゃ・きょうちんにょ)《8人の占師の一人としてシュッドーダナに招かれた際, 釈迦が必ず仏となると予言した。釈迦の最初の弟子》

□ **Kosala** 图コーサラ国《古代インドの王国》

□ **Kusinara** 图クシナラ《村の名》

L

□ **lady** 图婦人, 夫人, 淑女, 奥さん

□ **lake** 图湖, 湖水, 池

□ **lakeside** 图湖畔

□ **lamb** 图子羊 (の肉)

□ **lamp** 图ランプ, 灯火

□ **land** 图陸地, 土地

□ **language** 图言語, 言葉, 国語, ~語, 専門語

□ **lap** 图ひざ

□ **large** 形①大きい, 広い ②大勢の, 多量の

□ **last** 形①《the -》最後の ②この前の, 先~ ③最新の **the last time** この前~したとき 图《the -》最後 (のもの), 終わり **at last** ついに, とうとう 動続く, 持ちこたえる

□ **late** 形①遅い, 後期の ②最近の ③《the -》故~

□ **later** 形もっと遅い, もっと後の 副後で, 後ほど

□ **laugh** 動笑う **laugh at** ~を見て［聞いて］笑う

□ **law** 图法, 法律

□ **lay** 動lie (横たわる) の過去

□ **lead** 動導く, 案内する

□ **leader** 图指導者, リーダー

□ **learn** 動学ぶ, 習う, 教わる, 知識［経験］を得る

□ **leave** 動①出発する, 去る ②残す, 置き忘れる ③(~を…の) ままにしておく ④ゆだねる **leave behind** あとにする, ~を置き去りにする **leave for** ~に向かって出発する **leave in** ~をそのままにしておく **leave out** 抜かす, 除外する **leave ~ alone** ~をそっとしておく **leave ~ for …** …を~のために残しておく

□ **leaves** 图leaf (葉) の複数

□ **leaving** 形出発する, 別れの

□ **less** 形little (少しの) の比較級 **less and less** だんだん少なく~, ますます~でなく

□ **lesson** 图①授業, 学科, 課, けいこ ②教訓, 戒め

□ **let** 動(人に~) させる, (~するのを) 許す, (~をある状態に) する **let down** 期待を裏切る, 失望させる **let**

go of ～から手を離す **let us** どうか
私たちに～させてください

- [ ] **level** 图水準
- [ ] **lie** 動①うそをつく ②横たわる, 寝る ③(ある状態に)ある, 存在する 图うそ, 詐欺 **tell a lie** うそをつく
- [ ] **life** 图①生命, 生物 ②一生, 生涯, 人生 ③生活, 暮らし, 世の中 **all one's life** ずっと, 生まれてから **back to life** 生き返る, 息を吹き返す **for the rest of life** 死ぬまで
- [ ] **lifeless** 形①生物の住まない ②生命のない ③活力のない
- [ ] **light** 图光, 明かり
- [ ] **like** 好む, 好きである **would like** ～がほしい 副～に似ている, ～のような **like this** このような, こんなふうに **look like** ～のように見える, ～に似ている
- [ ] **limit** 图限界, 《-s》範囲, 境界 動制限[限定]する
- [ ] **limited** 形限られた, 限定の
- [ ] **line** 图線, 糸 **line of** ～の系統, 血筋
- [ ] **link** 图①(鎖の)輪 ②リンク ③相互[因果]関係
- [ ] **lion** 图ライオン **lion posture** 獅子臥(ししが)《右脇を下にする臥法》
- [ ] **listen** 動《-to ～》～を聞く, ～に耳を傾ける
- [ ] **little** 形①小さい, 幼い ②少しの, 短い ③ほとんど～ない, 《a-》少しはある 图少し(しか), 少量 副全然～ない, 《a-》少しはある
- [ ] **live** 動住む, 暮らす, 生きている
- [ ] **livelihood** 图生計, 暮らし, 生活 **right livelihood** 正命(しょうみょう)《正しい生活》
- [ ] **lively** 形①元気のよい, 活発な ②鮮やかな, 強烈な, 真に迫った
- [ ] **lives** life (生命)の複数
- [ ] **living** 動live (住む)の現在分詞 图生計, 生活 ①生きている, 現存の ②使用されている ③そっくりの

- [ ] **local** 形地方の, ある場所[土地]の
- [ ] **loka** 图ローカ, 世間, 世俗《サンスクリット語で「滅すべきもの」の意味》
- [ ] **lonely** 形①孤独な, 心さびしい ②ひっそりした, 人里離れた
- [ ] **long** 形①長い, 長期の ②《長さ・距離・時間などを示す語句を伴って》～の長さ[距離・時間]の **as long as** ～する以上は, ～である限りは **before long** やがて, まもなく **long ago** ずっと前に, 昔 副長い間, ずっと **all night long** 一晩中
- [ ] **longer** 熟**no longer** もはや～でない[～しない] **not ～ any longer** もはや～でない[～しない]
- [ ] **look** 動①見る ②(～に)見える, (～の)顔つきをする ③注意する ④《間投詞のように》ほら, ねえ **look after** ～の世話をする, ～に気をつける **look around** まわりを見回す **look for** ～を探す **look like** ～のように見える, ～に似ている **look up** 見上げる, 調べる **look up to** ～を仰ぎ見る 图①一見, 目つき ②外観, 外見, 様子 **take a look at** ～をちょっと見る
- [ ] **Lord** 图君主, 神, わが主
- [ ] **lose** 動①失う, 迷う, 忘れる ②負ける, 失敗する
- [ ] **loss** 图①損失(額・物), 損害, 浪費 ②失敗, 敗北
- [ ] **lost** 動lose (失う)の過去, 過去分詞 形①失った, 負けた ②道に迷った, 困った ③没頭している
- [ ] **lot** 图たくさん, たいへん, 《a-of ～/-s of～》たくさんの
- [ ] **lotus** 图ハス(蓮)《植物》 **lotus position** 蓮華座, 結跏趺坐(けっかふざ)《あぐらをかくように脚を交差させて, 一方の足首を他方の太股の上に置く座り方》
- [ ] **loud** 形大声の, 騒がしい
- [ ] **loudly** 副大声で, 騒がしく
- [ ] **love** 图愛, 愛情, 思いやり 動愛する, 恋する, 大好きである

□ **lover** 名 ①愛人, 恋人 ②愛好者

□ **loving** 動 love (愛する) の現在分詞
形 愛する, 愛情のこもった

□ **lower** 形 もっと低い, 下級の, 劣った 動 下げる, 低くする

□ **loyal** 形 忠実な, 誠実な

□ **Lumbini** 名 ルンビニ (藍毘尼) 《ネパールの南部タライ平原にある小さな村。釈迦の生誕地》 **Lumbini Garden** ルンビニの花園《摩耶夫人が里帰りの途中に休み釈迦を出産した場所》

□ **lunar** 形 月の, 月面の **lunar year** 太陰年

□ **lunch** 名 昼食, ランチ, 軽食

□ **luxury** 名 豪華さ, 贅沢 (品)

□ **lying** 動 lie (うそをつく・横たわる) の現在分詞 形 横になっている

M

□ **made** 動 make (作る) の過去, 過去分詞 形 作った, 作られた

□ **madhyama** 名 マディヤーマ《中庸, 中道の教え》

□ **Magadha** 名 マガダ国《古代インドにおける十六大国の一つ》

□ **magical** 形 ①魔法の力による ②魅惑的な

□ **magnificent** 形 壮大な, 壮麗な, すばらしい

□ **Mahamaya** 名 マーヤー夫人, 摩耶夫人 (まやぶにん) 《釈迦の生母》

□ **Mahamoggallana** 名 マハーモッガッラーナ, 目連《釈迦の十大弟子の一人》

□ **maid** 名 お手伝い, メイド

□ **make** 動 ①作る, 得る ②行う, (〜に) なる ③ (〜を…に) する, (〜を…) させる **make a mistake** 間違いをする **make fun of** 〜を物笑いの種にする, からかう **make it**

possible for 〜 to … 〜が…できるようにする **make sense** 意味をなす, よくわかる **make sure** 確かめる, 確認する **make up for** 償う, 〜の埋め合わせをする **make 〜 into** 〜を…に仕立てる **make 〜 out of** … 〜を…から作る

□ **mala** 名 花輪《サンスクリット語》

□ **man** 名 男性, 人, 人類

□ **Manat** 名 マナート《イスラム教以前の時代に崇められていた女神》

□ **many** 形 多数の, たくさんの **as many as** 〜もの数の **so many** 非常に多くの

□ **Mara** 名 マーラ《釈迦が悟りを開く禅定に入った時に, 瞑想を妨げるために現れたとされる悪魔, 魔神》

□ **march** 動 行進する [させる], 進展する

□ **marga** 名 マルガ《救済への道》

□ **mark** 名 印, 記号, 跡

□ **married** 動 marry (結婚する) の過去, 過去分詞 形 結婚した, 既婚の

□ **marry** 動 結婚する

□ **Mary** 名 ①マリア《イエスの母》②マルヤム (マリア) 《イーサー (ナザレのイエス) の母》

□ **Mary Magdalene** マグダラのマリア《イエスの弟子となるマグダラ出身の女性》

□ **master** 名 主人, 雇い主, 師, 名匠

□ **mat** 名 マット, 敷物

□ **material** 形 物質の

□ **matter** 名 物, 事, 事件, 問題 **What's the matter?** どうしたんですか。

□ **Matthew** 名 マタイ《十二使徒の一人; 新約聖書の「マタイによる福音書」の著者》

□ **may** 助 ①〜かもしれない ②〜してもよい, 〜できる **May I 〜?** 〜してもよいですか。《M-》5月

□ **Maysara** 名 メイサラ《ハディージ

A
B
C
D
E
F
G
H
I
J
K
L
M
N
O
P
Q
R
S
T
U
V
W
X
Y
Z

ャの召使の1人》

- □ **me** 代 私を[に]
- □ **meal** 名 食事
- □ **mean** 動 ①意味する ②(〜のつもりで) 言う, 意図する ③〜するつもりである
- □ **meaning** 名 ①意味, 趣旨 ②重要性
- □ **meant** 動 mean (意味する)の過去, 過去分詞
- □ **Mecca** 名 マッカ(メッカ)《サウジアラビア西部の都市。ムハンマドの生地》
- □ **Meccan** 名 マッカの人
- □ **Medina** 名 マディーナ (メディナ)《マッカに次ぐイスラム第2の聖地》
- □ **Medinat al-Nabi** 預言者の町《アラビア語》
- □ **meditate** 動 深く考える, 瞑想する
- □ **meditation** 名 瞑想, 黙想
- □ **meet** 動 ①会う, 知り合いになる ②合流する, 交わる ③(条件などに)達する, 合う
- □ **meeting** 名 ①集まり, ミーティング, 面会 ②競技会 **hold a meeting** 会議を開く
- □ **melt** 動 ①溶ける, 溶かす ②(感情が)和らぐ, 次第に消え去る
- □ **member** 名 一員, メンバー
- □ **men** 名 man (男性)の複数
- □ **merchant** 名 商人, 貿易商
- □ **mercy** 名 ①情け, 哀れみ, 慈悲 ②ありがたいこと, 幸運
- □ **message** 名 伝言, (作品などに込められた) メッセージ
- □ **messenger** 名 使者, (伝言・小包などの) 配達人, 伝達者
- □ **met** 動 meet (会う)の過去, 過去分詞
- □ **middle** 名 中間, 最中 **in the middle of** 〜の真ん中[中ほど]に

形 中間の, 中央の

- □ **might** 助 《mayの過去》①〜かもしれない ②〜してもよい, 〜できる
- □ **mile** 名 ①マイル《長さの単位。1,609m》②(-s)かなりの距離
- □ **milk** 名 牛乳, ミルク
- □ **million** 名 ①100万 ②《-s》数百万, 多数 形 ①100万の ②多数の
- □ **mind** 名 ①心, 精神, 考え ②知性
- □ **mine** 代 私のもの
- □ **miserable** 形 みじめな, 哀れな
- □ **mistake** 名 誤り, 誤解, 間違い **make a mistake** 間違いをする
- □ **modest** 形 控えめな, 謙虚な
- □ **moment** 名 ①瞬間, ちょっとの間 ②(特定の) 時, 時期 **at that moment** その時に, その瞬間に
- □ **monastery** 名 修道院, 僧院
- □ **money** 名 金, 通貨
- □ **monk** 名 修道士, 僧
- □ **month** 名 月, 1カ月
- □ **mood** 名 気分, 機嫌, 雰囲気, 憂うつ
- □ **moon** 名 月, 月光
- □ **moonlight** 名 月明かり, 月光
- □ **more** 形 ①もっと多くの ②それ以上の, 余分の 副 もっと, さらに多く, いっそう **more and more** ますます **more than** 〜以上 **once more** もう一度 **the more 〜 the more …** 〜すればするほどますます…
- □ **morning** 名 朝, 午前 **one morning** ある朝
- □ **Moses** 名 ①モーセ《古代イスラエルの民族指導者》②ムーサー(モーセ)《預言者。イスラム教における呼称》
- □ **mosque** 名 モスク, イスラム教寺院
- □ **most** 形 ①最も多い ②たいていの, 大部分の 副 最も (多く)
- □ **mother** 名 母, 母親

- □ **mount** 图山
- □ **Mount Arafat** アラファト山《マッカ東方にある花崗岩でできた山》
- □ **Mount of Olives** オリーブ山《エルサレム東郊にある丘陵》
- □ **Mount Safa** サファー《マッカにある小さな丘》
- □ **mountain** 图 ①山 ②《the ~ M-s》山脈
- □ **mountain of Thawr** サウル山《マッカの西南にある山》
- □ **mouth** 图 ①口 ②言葉, 発言
- □ **move** 動 ①動く, 動かす ②感動させる ③引っ越す, 移動する **move around** ～をあちこち動かす **move on** 先に進む **move to** ～に引っ越す
- □ **much** 形 (量・程度が) 多くの, 多量の **as much as** ～と同じだけ **too much** 過度の 副 ①とても, たいへん ②《比較級・最上級を修飾して》ずっと, はるかに
- □ **Muhammad** 图ムハンマド(・イブン = アブドゥッラーフ)《イスラム教の開祖》
- □ **murder** 動殺す
- □ **murderer** 图殺人犯
- □ **music** 图音楽, 楽曲
- □ **Muslim** 图イスラム教徒, ムスリム 形イスラム教[文明]の, ムスリム人の
- □ **must** 動 ①～しなければならない ②～に違いない
- □ **mustard** 图マスタード
- □ **my** 代私の
- □ **myself** 代私自身

N

- □ **nail** 動くぎを打つ, くぎづけにする
- □ **Nalagiri** 图ナーラーギリ《象の名。デーヴァダッタが酒に酔わせて釈迦を襲わせた》
- □ **name** 图名前 動名前をつける
- □ **Nanda** 图ナンダ, 難陀《釈迦の異母兄弟で, 弟子の一人》
- □ **nation** 图国, 国家,《the – 》国民
- □ **natural** 形 ①自然の, 天然の ②生まれつきの, 天性の ③当然な
- □ **Nazareth** 图ナザレ《イスラエル北部の地名》
- □ **near** 前～の近くに, ～のそばに 副近くに, 親密で **get near** 接近する
- □ **nearby** 形近くの, 間近の 副近くで, 間近で
- □ **nearly** 副 ①近くに, 親しく ②ほとんど, あやうく
- □ **necessary** 形必要な, 必然の
- □ **neck** 图首
- □ **need** 動 (～を) 必要とする, 必要である
- □ **neighbor** 图隣人, 隣り合うもの
- □ **nephew** 图おい(甥)
- □ **Neranjara, River** ネーランジャラー川, 尼連禅河 (にれんぜんが)《インド, ビハール州ブッダガヤーの東を流れる川》
- □ **nervous** 形 ①神経の ②神経質な, おどおどした
- □ **nest** 图巣
- □ **net** 图網, 網状のもの
- □ **never** 副決して[少しも～]ない, 一度も[二度と]～ない
- □ **new** 形 ①新しい, 新規の ②新鮮な, できたての
- □ **newborn** 形生まれたばかりの
- □ **news** 图報道, ニュース, 便り, 知らせ
- □ **next** 形 ①次の, 翌～ ②隣の **next to** ～のとなりに, ～の次に 副 ①次に ②隣に
- □ **niece** 图めい(姪)
- □ **night** 图夜, 晩 **all night long** 一晩中 **the night before** 前の晩

- □ **nightfall** 图 夕暮れ
- □ **nighttime** 图 夜間
- □ **ninth** 图 第9番目 (の人 [物]), 9日 图 第9番目の
- □ **nirvana** 图 ニルバーナ, 涅槃 (ねはん), 解脱《迷いや煩悩 (ぼんのう) や執着を断ち切り, 悟りに到達して, いっさいの苦・束縛・輪廻から解放された最高の境地》
- □ **no** 副 ①いいえ, いや ②少しも〜ない **no longer** もはや〜でない [〜しない] 形 〜がない, 少しも〜ない, 〜どころでない, 〜禁止 图 否定, 拒否
- □ **no one** 代 誰も [一人も] 〜ない **no one else** 他の誰一人として〜しない
- □ **noble** 形 気高い, 高貴な, りっぱな, 高貴な 图 貴族
- □ **nobody** 代 誰も [1人も] 〜ない
- □ **noise** 图 騒音, 騒ぎ, 物音
- □ **non-Muslim** 图 非イスラム教徒
- □ **none** 代 (〜の) 何も [誰も・少しも] …ない
- □ **nonsense** 图 ばかげたこと, ナンセンス
- □ **normal** 形 普通の, 平均の, 標準的な
- □ **normally** 副 普通は, 通常は
- □ **north** 图《the−》北, 北部 形 北の, 北からの
- □ **northern** 形 北の, 北向きの, 北からの
- □ **not** 副 〜でない, 〜しない **not always** 必ずしも〜であるとは限らない **not 〜 any longer** もはや〜でない [〜しない] **not 〜 but …** 〜ではなくて…
- □ **nothing** 代 何も〜ない [しない]
- □ **notice** 图 ①注意 ②通知 ③公告 動 ①気づく, 認める ②通告する
- □ **now** 副 ①今 (では), 現在 ②今すぐに ③では, さて **now that** 今や

〜だから, 〜からには 图 今, 現在 **by now** 今のところ, 今ごろまでには **here and now** 今この場で **right now** 今すぐに, たった今 形 今の, 現在の

- □ **nowhere** 副 どこにも〜ない
- □ **nurse** 图 ①看護師 [人] ②乳母
- □ **Nusayba** 图 ヌサイバ (・ビント・カアブ)《イスラムに改宗した初期の女性の1人》

O

- □ **oasis** 图 オアシス, 憩いの場
- □ **obey** 動 服従する, (命令などに) 従う
- □ **obligation** 图 義務, (社会的) 責任
- □ **ocean** 图 海, 大洋,《the 〜 O-》〜洋
- □ **of** 前 ①《所有・所属・部分》〜の, 〜に属する ②《性質・特徴・材料》〜の, 〜製の ③《部分》〜のうち ④《分離・除去》〜から **of one's own** 自分自身の **of the time** 当時の, 当節の
- □ **of course** もちろん, 当然
- □ **off** 副 ①離れて ②はずれて ③止まって ④休んで 形 ①離れて ②季節はずれの ③休みの 前 〜を離れて, 〜をはずれて, (値段が) 〜引きの **cut off** 切断する, 切り離す **get off** (〜から) 降りる **go off** ①出かける, 去る, 出発する ②始める, 突然〜しだす ③(電気が) 消える **hurry off** 急いで立ち去る, 急いで出掛ける **run off** 走り去る, 逃げ去る **set off** 出発する, 発射する **take off** (衣服を) 脱ぐ, 取り去る, 〜を取り除く, 離陸する, 出発する
- □ **offer** 動 申し出る, 申し込む, 提供する
- □ **offering** 图 (神への) ささげ物, 奉納の品
- □ **official** 形 公式の, 正式の

□ **often** 副 しばしば, たびたび

□ **oh** 間 ああ, おや, まあ

□ **oil** 名 油, 石油

□ **old** 形 ①年取った, 老いた ②〜歳の ③古い, 昔の **old age** 老齢

□ **Olives, Mount of** オリーブ山 《エルサレム東郊にある丘陵》

□ **on** 前 ①《場所・接触》〜(の上)に ②《日・時》〜に, 〜と同時に, 〜のすぐ後で ③《関係・従事》〜に関して, 〜について, 〜して 副 ①身につけて, 上に ②前へ, 続けて **climb on** 〜の上によじ登る **depend on** 〜をあてにする, 〜しだいである **from then on** それ以来 **go on** 続く, 続ける, 進み続ける, 起こる, 発生する **move on** 先に進む **on earth** 地球上で, この世で **on one's way** 途中で **on the ground** 地面に **on the way** 途中で **put on** ①〜を身につける, 着る ②〜を…の上に置く **set on fire** 火をつける **sit on** 〜の上に乗る, 〜の上に乗って動けないようにする **take someone on a business trip** (人)を出張に連れて行く **turn one's back on** 〜に背中を向ける, 〜を見捨てる **walk on** 歩き続ける

□ **once** 副 ①一度, 1回 ②かつて **once more** もう一度

□ **one** 名 1(の数字), 1人[個] **each one** 各自 **no one** 誰も[一人も]〜ない **no one else** 他の誰一人として〜しない **one of** 〜の1つ[人] **this one** これ, こちら 形 ①1の, 1人[個]の ②ある〜 ③《the-》唯一の **in one place** 一ヶ所に **one day** (過去の)ある日, (未来の)いつか **one morning** ある朝 代 ①(一般の)人, ある物 ②一方, 片方 ③〜なもの

□ **only** 形 唯一の 副 ①単に, 〜にすぎない, ただ〜だけ ②やっと

□ **onto** 前 〜の上へ[に]

□ **open** 形 ①開いた, 広々とした ②公開された **open air** 戸外, 野外 動 ①開く, 始まる ②広がる, 広げる ③打ち明ける **open up** 広がる, 広げ

る, 開く, 開ける

□ **openly** 副 率直に, 公然と

□ **opinion** 名 意見, 見識, 世論, 評判

□ **or** 接 ①〜か…, または ②さもないと ③すなわち, 言い換えると

□ **orange** 名 オレンジ 形 オレンジ色の

□ **order** 名 ①順序 ②整理, 整頓 ③命令, 注文(品) 動 ①(〜するよう)命じる, 注文する ②整頓する, 整理する

□ **originally** 副 ①元は, 元来 ②独創的に

□ **orphan** 孤児, みなし児

□ **other** 形 ①ほかの, 異なった ②(2つのうち)もう一方の, (3つ以上のうち)残りの 代 ①ほかの人[物] ②《the-》残りの人 **each other** お互いに

□ **our** 代 私たちの

□ **ourselves** 代 私たち自身

□ **out** 副 ①外へ[に], 不在で, 離れて ②世に出て ③消えて ④すっかり 形 ①外の, 遠く離れた ②公表された **be out** 外に出て 前 〜から外へ[に] **call out** 叫ぶ, 呼び出す, 声を掛ける **come out** 出てくる, 出掛ける, 姿を現す, 発行される **come out of** 〜から出てくる, 〜をうまく乗り越える **cry out** 叫ぶ **find out** 見つけ出す, 気がつく, 知る, 調べる, 解明する **get out** ①外に出る, 出て行く, 逃げ出す ②取り出す, 抜き出す **go out** 外出する, 外へ出る **hold out** 差し出す, (腕を)伸ばす **leave out** 抜かす, 除外する **make 〜 out of** … 〜を…から作る **out of** ①〜から外へ, 〜から抜け出して ②〜から作り出して, 〜を材料として ③〜の範囲外に, 〜から離れて ④(ある数)の中から **pour out** どっと出てくる, 〜に注ぎだす, 吐き出す **pull out** 引き抜く, 引き出す, 取り出す **put out** ①外に出す, (手など)を(差し)出す ②(明かり・火を)消す **reach out** 手を伸ばす **run out of** 〜が不足する, 〜を使い果たす **set out** 出発する **shout**

out 大声で叫ぶ **step out** 外へ出る **take out** 取り出す, 取り外す, 連れ出す, 持って帰る **take out of** 〜から出す, 〜に連れ出す **way out** 出口, 逃げ道, 脱出方法, 解決法

□ **outside** 图外部, 外側 形外部の, 外側の, 外側へ, 外側に 前〜の外に [で・の・へ], 〜の範囲を越えて

□ **over** 前①〜の上の[に], 〜を一面に覆って ②〜を越えて, 〜以上に, 〜よりまさって ③〜の向こう側の[に] ④〜の間 副①上に, ずっと **all over** 〜中で, 全体に亘って, 〜の至る所で **come over to** 〜にやって来る **have power over** 〜を思いのままに操る力を持っている **rule over** 治める, 統御する **turn over** ひっくり返る [返す], (ページを)めくる, 思いめぐらす, 引き渡す **walk over** 〜の方に歩いていく ②上部の, 上位の, 過多の ②終わって, すんで **be over** 終わる

□ **overcome** 動勝つ, 打ち勝つ, 克服する

□ **own** 形自身の **of one's own** 自分自身の

P

□ **padmasana** 图パドマーサナ, 結跏趺坐 (けっかふざ), 蓮華座《あぐらをかくように脚を交差させて, 一方の足首を他方の太股の上に置く座り方》

□ **pagoda** 图仏塔

□ **paid** 動pay (払う) の過去, 過去分詞

□ **pain** 图①痛み, 苦悩 ②《-s》骨折り, 苦労 動苦痛を与える, 痛む

□ **painful** 形①痛い, 苦しい, 痛ましい ②骨の折れる, 困難な

□ **pair** 图 (2つから成る) 一対, 一組, ペア

□ **palace** 图宮殿, 大邸宅

□ **palm** 图手のひら (状のもの)

□ **paper** 图紙

□ **paralyzed** 形まひした

□ **parent** 图《-s》両親

□ **part** 图①部分, 割合 ②役目

□ **pass** 動過ぎる, 通る **pass by** 〜のそばを通る [通り過ぎる] **pass through** 〜を通る, 通行する

□ **Passover** 图過越 (すぎこし)《ユダヤ教の祭日の一つ》

□ **past** 形過去の, この前の 图過去(の出来事) 前《時間・場所》〜を過ぎて, 〜を越して 副通り越して, 過ぎて

□ **path** 图①(踏まれてできた)小道, 歩道 ②進路, 通路 **eightfold path** 八正道 (はっしょうどう)《仏教において涅槃に至るための8つの実践徳目である正見, 正思惟, 正語, 正業, 正命, 正精進, 正念, 正定のこと》

□ **pause** 图①(活動の)中止, 休止 ②区切り

□ **Pava** 图パヴァ《地名。現在のパドラウナ (Padrauna)》

□ **pay** 動支払う, 払う **pay a visit** 〜を訪問する

□ **peace** 图①平和, 和解,《the -》治安 ②平穏, 静けさ **in peace** 平和のうちに, 安心して

□ **peaceful** 形平和な, 穏やかな

□ **peaceful-looking** 形平穏に見える, 落ち着いたように見える

□ **peacefully** 副平和に, 穏やかに

□ **pen** 图ペン

□ **peninsula** 图半島

□ **people** 图①(一般に)人々 ②民衆, 世界の人々, 国民, 民族 ③人間 **fishers of people** 人間の漁をする (人を集める)漁師

□ **perfect** 形①完璧な, 完全な ②純然たる

□ **perfectly** 副完全に, 申し分なく

□ **perfume** 图香り, 香水

□ **perhaps** 副たぶん, ことによると

□ **person** 名①人 ②人格, 人柄 **in person** (本人) 自ら, 自身で

□ **perspective** 名①遠近法 ②観点 ③見通し **right perspective** 正見(しょうけん)《正しいものの見方》

□ **Peter** 名ペトロ《イエスがシモンに与えた名前。「岩・石」の意味》**Simon Peter** シモン・ペトロ《十二使徒の一人》

□ **Pharisee** 名パリサイ(派の)人《古代ユダヤで律法の形式を重んじた保守派の人》

□ **Philip** 名フィリポ《十二使徒の一人》

□ **physically** 副①自然法則上, 物理的に ②肉体的に, 身体的に

□ **pick** 動①(花・果実などを)摘む, もぐ ②選ぶ, 精選する ③つつく, つついて穴をあける, ほじくり出す ④(～を)摘み取る **pick up** 拾い上げる

□ **piece** 名①一片, 部分 ②1個, 1本 ③作品

□ **pilgrim** 名①巡礼者, 旅人 ②最初の移住者

□ **pilgrimage** 名巡礼

□ **place** 名①場所, 建物 ②余地, 空間 ③《one's-》家, 部屋 **in one place** 一ヶ所に **in place of** ～の代わりに **take one's place** (人と)交代する, (人)の代わりをする, 後任になる **take place** 行われる, 起こる 動①置く, 配置する ②任命する, 任じる

□ **plain** 形①明白な, はっきりした ②簡素な ③平らな ④不細工な, 平凡な

□ **plan** 名計画, 設計(図), 案 動計画する

□ **plant** 名植物, 草木 動植えつける, すえつける

□ **play** 動遊ぶ, 競技する

□ **please** 動喜ばす, 満足させる 間どうぞ, お願いします

□ **pleased** 形喜んだ, 気に入った

□ **plow** 名鋤, プラウ《農具》

□ **point** 名①先, 先端 ②点 ③地点, 時点, 箇所 ④《the-》要点

□ **poison** 名毒, 毒薬

□ **polite** 形ていねいな, 礼儀正しい, 洗練された

□ **pollution** 名汚染, 公害

□ **Pontius Pilate** ポンテオ・ピラト《ローマ帝国のユダヤ属州総督》

□ **poor** 形①貧しい, 乏しい, 粗末な, 貧弱な ②劣った, へたな ③不幸な, 哀れな, 気の毒な

□ **popular** 形①人気のある, 流行の ②一般的な, 一般向きの

□ **porridge** 名かゆ, ポリッジ《穀物を水などで煮たかゆ状のもの》

□ **position** 名位置, 場所, 姿勢

□ **possible** 形①可能な ②ありうる, 起こりうる **as ～ as possible** できるだけ～ **make it possible for ～ to …** ～が…できるようにする

□ **posture** 名姿勢

□ **pour** 動①注ぐ, 浴びせる ②流れ出る, 流れ込む ③ざあざあ降る **pour out** どっと出てくる, ～に注ぎだす, 吐き出す

□ **power** 名力, 能力, 才能, 勢力, 権力 **have power over** ～を思いのままに操る力を持っている

□ **powerful** 形力強い, 実力のある, 影響力のある

□ **practice** 動実行する, 練習[訓練]する

□ **praise** 動ほめる, 賞賛する

□ **Prajapati Gotami** プラジャーパティー・ゴータミー, 摩訶波闍波提(まかはじゃはだい)《釈迦の叔母であり養母》

□ **pray** 動祈る, 懇願する **pray for** ～のために祈る **pray to God for** ～を神に祈る

□ **prayer** 名①祈り, 祈願(文) ②祈る人

161

□ **preaching** 名 説教

□ **prediction** 名 予言, 予報, 予測

□ **prepare** 動 ①準備 [用意] をする ②覚悟する [させる]

□ **presence** 名 ①存在すること ②出席, 態度

□ **present** 名 ①《the –》現在 ②贈り物, プレゼント

□ **price** 名 ①値段, 代価 ②《-s》物価, 相場

□ **priest** 名 聖職者, 牧師, 僧侶

□ **prince** 名 王子, プリンス

□ **Prince Jeta** ジェータ (祇陀) 太子《コーサラ国の王子》

□ **principle** 名 ①原理, 原則 ②道義, 正道

□ **prison** 名 ①刑務所, 監獄 ②監禁

□ **prisoner** 名 囚人, 捕虜

□ **probably** 副 たぶん, あるいは

□ **problem** 名 問題, 難問

□ **produce** 動 生産する, 製造する

□ **promise** 名 約束 動 約束する

□ **prophet** 名 予言者, 預言者

□ **protect** 動 保護する, 防ぐ

□ **province** 名 ①州, 省 ②地方, 田舎 ③範囲, 領域

□ **pull** 動 ①引く, 引っ張る ②引きつける **pull in** 引っ込める, (網, 釣り糸を) 引く **pull out** 引き抜く, 引き出す, 取り出す

□ **punish** 動 罰する, ひどい目にあわせる **be punished for** ~によって罰せられる

□ **punishment** 名 ①罰, 処罰 ②罰を受けること

□ **pure** 形 ①純粋な, 混じりけのない ②罪のない, 清い

□ **purple** 形 紫色の 名 紫色

□ **purpose** 名 目的, 意図, 決意

□ **push** 動 ①押す, 押し進む, 押し進める ②進む, 突き出る **push down** 押し倒す

□ **put** 動 ①置く, のせる ②入れる, つける ③ (ある状態に) する ④putの過去, 過去分詞 **put an end to** ~に終止符を打つ, ~を終わらせる, ~に決着をつける **put down** 下に置く, 下ろす **put in** ~の中に入れる **put on** ①~を身につける, 着る ②~を…の上に置く **put out** ①外に出す, (手など) を (差し) 出す ②(明かり・火を) 消す **put up** ~を上げる, 揚げる, 建てる, 飾る **put ~ into …** ~を…の状態にする, ~を…に突っ込む

Q

□ **Qasim** 名 カースィム《ムハンマドの息子》

□ **queen** 名 女王, 王妃

□ **question** 名 質問, 疑問, 問題 動 ①質問する ②調査する ③疑う

□ **quickly** 副 敏速に, 急いで

□ **quiet** 形 ①静かな, 穏やかな, じっとした ②おとなしい, 無口な, 目立たない

□ **quietly** 副 ①静かに ②平穏に, 控えめに

□ **quite** 副 ①まったく, すっかり, 完全に ②かなり, ずいぶん ③ほとんど

□ **Qur'an** 名 クルアーン (コーラン)《イスラム教の聖典》

□ **Quraysh** 名 クライシュ族《当時マッカの支配権を握っていた商業貴族の部族》

□ **Qurayzah** 名 クライザ族《ヤスリブに住んでいたユダヤ教徒の部族》

R

□ **rag** 名 ぼろ切れ, 布きれ

□ **Rahula** 名 ラーフラ, 羅睺羅 (らごら)《釈迦の実子で, 十大弟子の一人》

WORD LIST

- [ ] **rain** 名 雨, 降雨 動 ①雨が降る ② 雨のように降る[降らせる]
- [ ] **raise** 動 ～を育てる
- [ ] **Rajagriha** 名 ラージャグリハ, 王舎城(おうしゃじょう)《マガダ国の首都》
- [ ] **Rama** 名 ラーマ《インドの叙事詩『ラーマーヤナ』の主人公。古代インドの伝説上の英雄》
- [ ] **Ramadan** 名 ラマダーン, 断食月《イスラム暦で9番目の月。この月は, 日の出から日没まで断食をする》
- [ ] **ran** 動 run (走る)の過去
- [ ] **rather** 副 ①むしろ, かえって ②かなり, いくぶん, やや ③それどころか逆に **rather than** ～よりむしろ
- [ ] **reach** 動 ①着く, 到着する, 届く ②手を伸ばして取る **reach out** 手を伸ばす
- [ ] **read** 動 読む, 読書する
- [ ] **ready** 形 用意[準備]ができた, まさに～しようとする, 今にも～せんばかりの **get ready** 用意[支度]をする
- [ ] **real** 形 実際の, 実在する, 本物の
- [ ] **reality** 名 現実, 実在, 真実(性)
- [ ] **realize** 動 理解する, 実現する
- [ ] **really** 副 本当に, 実際に, 確かに
- [ ] **reason** 名 ①理由 ②理性, 道理 **reason for** ～の理由
- [ ] **rebuild** 動 再建する, 改造する
- [ ] **receive** 動 ①受け取る, 受領する ②迎える, 迎え入れる
- [ ] **recite** 動 暗唱する, 復唱する, 物語る, 朗読する
- [ ] **red** 形 赤い 名 赤, 赤色
- [ ] **regular** 形 ①規則的な, 秩序のある ②定期的な, 一定の, 習慣的
- [ ] **rein** 名 手綱, 拘束, 統制, 統御力, 支配権, 指揮権
- [ ] **relationship** 名 関係, 関連, 血縁関係
- [ ] **relative** 名 親戚, 同族

- [ ] **relax** 動 ①くつろがせる ②ゆるめる, 緩和する
- [ ] **relaxed** 動 relax (くつろがせる)の過去, 過去分詞 形 ①くつろいだ, ゆったりした ②ざっくばらんな
- [ ] **religion** 名 宗教, ～教, 信条
- [ ] **religious** 形 ①宗教の ②信心深い
- [ ] **remain** 動 ①残っている, 残る ②(～の)ままである[いる]
- [ ] **remaining** 形 残った, 残りの
- [ ] **remember** 動 思い出す, 覚えている, 忘れないでいる
- [ ] **remind** 動 思い出させる, 気づかせる
- [ ] **remove** 動 ①取り去る, 除去する ②(衣類を)脱ぐ
- [ ] **repeat** 動 繰り返す
- [ ] **reply** 動 答える, 返事をする, 応答する
- [ ] **report** 名 報告
- [ ] **rescue** 動 救う
- [ ] **respect** 名 ①尊敬, 尊重 ②注意, 考慮 動 尊敬[尊重]する
- [ ] **responsibility** 名 ①責任, 義務, 義理 ②負担, 責務
- [ ] **rest** 名 ①休息 ②安静 ③休止, 停止 ④《the -》残り **for the rest of life** 死ぬまで 動 ①休む, 眠る ②休止する, 静止する ③(～に)基づいている ④(～の)ままである
- [ ] **result** 名 結果, 成り行き, 成績
- [ ] **return** 動 帰る, 戻る, 返す 名 ①帰還, 返却 ②返答, 報告(書), 申告 **in return** お返しとして
- [ ] **reveal** 動 明らかにする, 暴露する, もらす
- [ ] **revelation** 名 ①明らかになること, 発覚, 暴露(されたもの), 新事実 ②啓示 **angel of revelation** 啓示の天使《神のことばを伝える天使》
- [ ] **revenge** 名 復讐
- [ ] **reward** 名 報酬, 償い, 応報

163

- □ **rice** 名米, 飯 **rice cake** 餅
- □ **rich** 形①富んだ, 金持ちの ②豊かな, 濃い, 深い 名裕福な人
- □ **riddle** 名謎
- □ **ride** 動乗る, 乗って行く, 馬に乗る
- □ **ridiculous** 形ばかげた, おかしい
- □ **right** 形①正しい ②適切な ③健全な ④右(側)の 副①まっすぐに, すぐに ②右(側)に ③ちょうど, 正確に **right now** 今すぐに, たった今 名①正しいこと ②権利 ③《the –》右, ライト ④《the R-》右翼
- □ **right attention** 正念(しょうねん)《正しい集中力》
- □ **right concentration** 正定(しょうじょう)《正しい精神統一》
- □ **right conduct** 正業(しょうごう)《正しい行い》
- □ **right endeavor** 正精進(しょうしょうじん)《正しい努力, 修養》
- □ **right intention** 正思惟(しょうしゆい)《正しい思考》
- □ **right livelihood** 正命(しょうみょう)《正しい生活》
- □ **right perspective** 正見(しょうけん)《正しいものの見方》
- □ **right speech** 正語(しょうご)《正しい言葉》
- □ **rise** 動①昇る, 上がる ②生じる
- □ **ritual** 名①儀式 ②行事 ③慣例
- □ **river** 名川
- □ **River Anoma** アノマ川《ネパール南部のカビラヴァストゥ近くの川》
- □ **River Jordan** ヨルダン川《イスラエルのフラ湖とガリラヤ湖を通って死海に注ぐ川》
- □ **River Neranjara** ネーランジャラー川, 尼連禅河(にれんぜんが)《インド, ビハール州ブッダガヤーの東を流れる川》
- □ **road** 名①道路, 道, 通り ②手段, 方法
- □ **robber** 名泥棒, 強盗
- □ **robe** 名①ローブ, 化粧着, 部屋着 ②《-s》式服, 法衣
- □ **rock** 名岩, 岸壁, 岩石
- □ **rode** 動 ride (乗る)の過去
- □ **role** 名①(劇などの)役 ②役割, 任務
- □ **roll** 動①転がる, 転がす ②(波などが)うねる, 横揺れする ③(時が)たつ
- □ **Roman** 形ローマ(人)の 名①ローマ人[市民] ②(ローマ)カトリック教
- □ **Roman coin** 古代ローマコイン《デナリウス(denarius)銀貨。ローマ皇帝の肖像が刻印されている》
- □ **Rome** 名ローマ《古代ローマ帝国の首都》
- □ **roof** 名屋根(のようなもの), 住居
- □ **room** 名①部屋 ②空間, 余地
- □ **root** 名根, 根元
- □ **rope** 名綱, なわ, ロープ
- □ **rose** 名①バラ(の花) ②バラ色 形バラ色の 動 rise (昇る)の過去
- □ **rose apple** 《植物》フトモモ
- □ **round** 形①丸い, 円形の ②ちょうど 副①回って ②周りに 前①~を回って ②~の周囲に
- □ **route** 名道, 道筋, 進路, 回路
- □ **royal** 形王の, 女王の, 国立の
- □ **rule** 名①規則, ルール ②支配 動支配する **rule over** 治める, 統御する
- □ **ruling** 形支配的な, 優勢な
- □ **run** 動①走る ②運行する ③(川が)流れる ④経営する **run away** 走り去る, 逃げ出す **run into** (思いがけず)~に出会う, ~に駆け込む, ~の中に走って入る **run off** 走り去る, 逃げ去る **run out of** ~が不足する, ~を使い果たす
- □ **Ruqayya** 名ルカイヤ《ムハンマド

164

の娘》
- □ **rush** 動 突進する, せき立てる

S

- □ **Sabbath** 名《the –》安息日
- □ **sacred** 形 神聖な, 厳粛な
- □ **sacrifice** 動（〜に）生け贄をささげる,（〜のために）犠牲になる
- □ **sad** 形 ①悲しい, 悲しげな ②惨めな, 不運な
- □ **sadden** 動（〜を）悲しませる
- □ **sadly** 副 悲しそうに, 不幸にも
- □ **sadness** 名 悲しみ, 悲哀
- □ **Safa, Mount** サファー《マッカにある小さな丘》
- □ **safe** 形 ①安全な, 危険のない ②用心深い, 慎重な
- □ **safely** 副 安全に, 間違いなく
- □ **said** 動 say（言う）の過去, 過去分詞
- □ **saint** 名 聖人, 聖徒
- □ **Sakya** 名 シャーキヤ《ヒマラヤ山麓にあった古代北インドの一部族・小国》
- □ **sala tree** サラソウジュ（沙羅双樹）《植物》
- □ **salvation** 名 救出, 救済, 救い
- □ **samatha** 名 サマタ瞑想《心を特定の対象に結びつけて集中する瞑想》
- □ **same** 形 ①同じ, 同様の ②前述の 副《the –》同様に
- □ **sand** 名 ①砂 ②《-s》砂漠, 砂浜
- □ **sandstorm** 名 砂嵐
- □ **sangha** 名 サンガ, 僧伽, 僧《男性の出家修行者である「比丘（びく）」と女性の出家修行者である「比丘尼（びくに）」の集団のこと》
- □ **Sariputta** 名 シャーリプトラ, 舎利弗（しゃりほつ）《釈迦の十大弟子の一人》

- □ **sat** 動 sit（座る）の過去, 過去分詞
- □ **satisfied** 形 満足した
- □ **save** 動 ①救う, 守る ②とっておく, 節約する
- □ **saw** 動 see（見る）の過去
- □ **say** 動 言う, 口に出す **say to oneself** ひとり言を言う, 心に思う
- □ **saying** 動 say（言う）の現在分詞
- □ **scare** 動 こわがらせる, おびえる
- □ **sceptre** 名 王笏（おうしゃく）《王権の象徴の杖》
- □ **sceptre-wielding** 形 王笏を振るう
- □ **scratch** 名 ひっかき傷, かくこと
- □ **scripture** 名《the S-》聖書
- □ **sea** 名 海,《the 〜 S, the S- of 〜》〜海
- □ **Sea of Galilee** ガリラヤ湖《イスラエル北東部。ヨルダン川につながる湖》
- □ **search** 動 捜し求める, 調べる 名 捜査, 探索, 調査
- □ **season** 名 季, 季節
- □ **seat** 名 席, 座席, 位置 **take a seat** 席にすわる
- □ **second** 名 ①第2（の人［物］）②（時間の）秒, 瞬時 形 第2の, 2番の 副 第2に 動 後援する, 支持する
- □ **secret** 形 ①秘密の, 隠れた ②神秘の, 不思議な 名 秘密, 神秘
- □ **sedition** 名（国家に対する反乱の）教唆, 扇動
- □ **seduce** 動 誘惑する, そそのかす, くどく
- □ **see** 動 ①見る, 見える, 見物する ②（〜と）わかる, 認識する, 経験する ③会う ④考える, 確かめる, 調べる ⑤気をつける **see 〜 as …** 〜を…と考える
- □ **seed** 名 種
- □ **seek** 動 捜し求める, 求める
- □ **seem** 動（〜に）見える,（〜のよう

THREE RELIGIOUS LEADERS: JESUS, BUDDHA, AND MUHAMMAD

□ **seen** 動 see (見る) の過去分詞

□ **self-indulgence** 名 わがまま, 身勝手

□ **self-indulgent** 形 わがままな, 身勝手な

□ **self-mortification** 名 自ら進んで苦行すること

□ **selfish** 形 わがままな, 自分本位の, 利己主義の

□ **sell** 動 売る, 売っている, 売れる

□ **Senani** 名 セナニ《村の名》

□ **send** 動 ①送る, 届ける ②手紙を出す ③(人を~に)行かせる ④《 – + 人 [物など] + ~ing》~を(ある状態に)する

□ **sense** 名 ①感覚, 感じ ②《-s》意識, 正気, 本性 ③常識, 分別, センス ④意味 **make sense** 意味をなす, よくわかる

□ **sent** 動 send (送る) の過去, 過去分詞

□ **seriously** 副 ①真剣に, まじめに ②重大に

□ **servant** 名 召使, 使用人, しもべ

□ **set** 動 ①置く, 当てる, つける ②整える, 設定する ③(太陽・月などが)沈む ④(~を…の状態に)する, させる ⑤setの過去, 過去分詞 **set off** 出発する, 発射する **set on fire** 火をつける **set out** 出発する

□ **seven** 名 7(の数字), 7人 [個] 形 7の, 7人 [個] の

□ **seventh** 名 第7番目 (の人・物), 7日 形 第7番目の

□ **several** 形 ①いくつかの ②めいめいの

□ **shadow** 名 ①影, 暗がり ②亡霊

□ **shake** 動 ①振る, 揺れる, 揺さぶる, 震える ②動揺させる

□ **shall** 助 ①《Iが主語で》~するだろう, ~だろう ②《I以外が主語で》(…

に) ~させよう, (…は) ~することになるだろう **Shall I ~?** (私が) ~しましょうか。

□ **share** 動 分配する, 共有する

□ **she** 代 彼女は [が]

□ **sheep** 名 羊

□ **shelter** 動 避難する, 隠れる

□ **shepherd** 名 ①羊飼い ②牧師

□ **shield** 名 盾, 防衛物

□ **shiver** 動 (寒さなどで) 身震いする, 震える

□ **shore** 名 岸, 海岸, 陸

□ **short** 形 ①短い ②背の低い ③不足している

□ **shot** 動 shoot (撃つ) の過去, 過去分詞

□ **should** 助 ~すべきである, ~したほうがよい **should have done** ~すべきだった (のにしなかった)《仮定法》

□ **shout** 動 叫ぶ, 大声で言う, どなりつける **shout out** 大声で叫ぶ

□ **shouting** 名 叫び

□ **show** 動 ①見せる, 示す, 見える ②明らかにする, 教える ③案内する **show ~ how to …** ~に…のやり方を示す

□ **shower** 動 にわか雨が降る, 雨のように注ぐ

□ **shown** 動 show (見せる) の過去分詞

□ **shrine** 名 廟, 聖堂, 神社

□ **Shwedagon Pagoda** シュエダゴン・パゴダ《ミャンマーのヤンゴン中心部に存在する寺院》

□ **sick** 形 ①病気の ②むかついて, いや気がさして

□ **sickness** 名 病気

□ **Siddhartha Gautama** ガウタマ・シッダールタ, 釈迦《仏教の開祖》

□ **side** 名 側, 横, そば, 斜面

□ **sign** 名 ①きざし, 徴候 ②跡 ③記

号 ④身振り, 合図, 看板 **動** ①署名する, サインする ②合図する

□ **silence** 名 沈黙, 無言, 静寂 **in silence** 黙って, 沈黙のうちに

□ **silver** 名 銀, 銀貨, 銀色 形 銀製の

□ **Simon** 名 ①シモン (・ペトロ)《十二使徒の一人》②熱心党のシモン《十二使徒の一人》

□ **Simon Peter** シモン・ペトロ《十二使徒の一人》

□ **simple** 形 ①単純な, 簡単な, 質素な ②単一の, 単独の ③普通の, ただの

□ **simply** 副 ①簡単に ②単に, ただ ③まったく, 完全に

□ **sin** 名 (道徳・宗教上の)罪

□ **since** 接 ①〜以来 ②〜だから 前 〜以来 副 それ以来

□ **sincerely** 副 真心をこめて

□ **single** 形 ①たった1つの ②1人用の, それぞれの ③独身の ④片道の

□ **sister** 名 姉妹, 姉, 妹

□ **sit** 動 ①座る, 腰掛ける ②止まる ③位置する **sit at the table** 食卓につく **sit on** 〜の上に乗る, 〜の上に乗って動けないようにする

□ **six** 名 6(の数字), 6人[個] 形 6の, 6人[個]の

□ **sixth** 名 第6番目(の人・物), 6日 形 第6番目の

□ **sixty** 名 60(の数字), 60人[個] 形 60の, 60人[個]の

□ **skin** 名 皮膚, 皮, 革(製品)

□ **skull** 名 頭蓋骨, 頭, 頭脳

□ **sky** 名 ①空, 天空, 大空 ②天気, 空模様, 気候

□ **slave** 名 奴隷

□ **sleep** 動 ①眠る, 寝る ②活動しない **go to sleep** 寝る

□ **sleeping** 形 眠っている, 休止している

□ **slowly** 副 遅く, ゆっくり

□ **small** 形 ①小さい, 少ない ②取るに足りない

□ **smile** 動 微笑する, にっこり笑う 名 微笑, ほほえみ

□ **snake** 名 ヘビ(蛇)

□ **so** 副 ①とても ②同様に, 〜もまた ③《先行する句・節の代用》そのように, そう **So be it.** それならそれでいい。**and so** そこで, それだから, それで **so many** 非常に多くの **so that** 〜するために, それで, 〜できるように **so 〜 that** …非常に〜なので… 接 ①だから, それで ②では, さて

□ **social** 形 ①社会の, 社会的な ②社交的な, 愛想のよい

□ **society** 名 社会, 世間

□ **soft** 形 ①柔らかい, 手ざわり[口あたり]のよい ②温和な, 落ち着いた ③(処分などが)厳しくない, 手ぬるい, 甘い **soft life** 安楽な生活

□ **softly** 副 柔らかに, 優しく, そっと

□ **soil** 名 土, 土地

□ **sold** 動 sell (売る)の過去, 過去分詞

□ **soldier** 名 兵士, 兵卒

□ **some** 形 ①いくつかの, 多少の ②ある, 誰か, 何か **some time** いつか, そのうち 副 約, およそ 代 ①いくつか ②ある人[物]たち

□ **somebody** 代 誰か, ある人

□ **someday** 副 いつか, そのうち

□ **someone** 代 ある人, 誰か

□ **something** 代 ①ある物, 何か ②いくぶん, 多少 **something to do** 何か〜すべきこと

□ **sometimes** 副 時々, 時たま

□ **son** 名 息子, 子弟, 〜の子 **Son of God** 神の子

□ **song** 名 歌, 詩歌, 鳴き声

□ **soon** 副 まもなく, すぐに, すみやかに **as soon as** 〜するとすぐ, 〜るや否や

□ **sore** 名 傷, ふれると痛いところ

167

□ **sorry** 形気の毒に [申し訳なく] 思う, 残念な

□ **sort** 名種類, 品質 **a sort of** 〜のようなもの, 一種の〜 **what sort of** どういう

□ **soul** 名①魂 ②精神, 心

□ **sound** 名音, 騒音, 響き, サウンド

□ **south** 名《the −》南, 南方, 南部 形南の, 南方 [南部] の

□ **southwest** 名南西 (部) 形南西の, 南西向きの 副南西へ, 南西から

□ **space** 名①空間, 宇宙 ②すき間, 余地, 場所, 間

□ **speak** 動話す, 言う, 演説する

□ **special** 形①特別の, 特殊の, 臨時の ②専門の

□ **specially** 副特別に

□ **speech** 名演説, 言語, 語 **right speech** 正語 (しょうご) 《正しい言葉》

□ **spend** 動① (金などを) 使う, 消費 [浪費] する ② (時を) 過ごす

□ **spent** 動 spend (使う) の過去, 過去分詞

□ **spider** 名クモ (蜘蛛)

□ **spike** 名大くぎ

□ **spirit** 名①霊 ②精神, 気力

□ **spiritual** 形精神の, 精神的な, 霊的な

□ **spiritually** 副精神的に, 霊的に

□ **spoke** 動 speak (話す) の過去

□ **spot** 名斑点, しみ

□ **spread** 動広がる, 広げる, 伸びる, 伸ばす

□ **spring** 名春

□ **stage** 名①舞台 ②段階

□ **stand** 動①立つ, 立たせる, 立っている, ある ②耐える, 立ち向かう **stand up** 立ち上がる

□ **stare** 動じっと [じろじろ] 見る

□ **start** 動①出発する, 始まる, 始め

る ②生じる, 生じさせる

□ **state** 名①あり様, 状態 ②国家, (アメリカなどの) 州 ③階層, 地位

□ **stay** 動①とどまる, 泊まる, 滞在する ②持続する, (〜の) ままでいる **stay away from** 〜から離れている **stay in** 家にいる, (場所) に泊まる, 滞在する **stay with** 〜の所に泊まる

□ **steady** 形①しっかりした, 安定した, 落ち着いた ②堅実な, まじめな

□ **steal** 動①盗む ②こっそりと手に入れる, こっそりと〜する

□ **step** 名①歩み, 1歩の (距離) ②段階 ③踏み段, 階段 **step out** 外へ出る 動歩む, 踏む

□ **stick** 名棒, 杖

□ **still** 副①まだ, 今でも ②それでも (なお) 形静止した, 静かな

□ **stomach** 名胃, 腹

□ **stone** 名石, 小石

□ **stood** 動 stand (立つ) の過去, 過去分詞

□ **stop** 動①やめる, やめさせる, 止める, 止まる ②立ち止まる **stop to** 〜しようと立ち止まる

□ **storm** 名嵐, 暴風雨

□ **story** 名物語, 話

□ **straight** 形副①一直線に, まっすぐに, 垂直に ②率直に

□ **strange** 形①知らない, 見 [聞き] 慣れない ②奇妙な, 変わった

□ **stranger** 名①見知らぬ人, 他人 ②不案内 [不慣れ] な人

□ **street** 名街路

□ **strength** 名①力, 体力 ②長所, 強み ③強度, 濃度

□ **stretch** 動引き伸ばす, 広がる, 広げる

□ **strict** 形厳しい, 厳密な

□ **strong** 形①強い, 堅固な, 強烈な ②濃い ③得意な

□ **student** 名学生, 生徒

□ **study** 動 ①勉強する，研究する ②調べる

□ **subdue** 動 征服する，抑える

□ **Subhadda** 名 スバッダ，須跋陀《釈迦の弟子の一人》

□ **submission** 名 服従，降伏

□ **substance** 名 ①物質，物 ②実質，中身，内容

□ **such** 形 ①そのような，このような ②そんなに，とても，非常に **such a** そのような **such as** たとえば～，～のような

□ **suddenly** 副 突然，急に

□ **Suddhodana** 名 シュッドーダナ，浄飯王（じょうぼんおう）《シャーキヤ族の王にして釈迦の実父》

□ **suffer** 動 ①(苦痛・損害などを) 受ける，こうむる ②(病気に) なる，苦しむ，悩む

□ **Sujata** 名 スジャータ《釈迦が悟る直前に乳がゆを供養し命を救った娘》

□ **sukaramaddava** 名 スーカラ・マッダヴァ《チュンダが釈迦に差し出した料理の名。スーカラとは「野豚」，マッダヴァとは「柔らかい」の意味。豚が好む種のキノコを使った料理と言われている》

□ **Sumayya** 名 スマイヤ（・ビント・ハッバー）《ウンマの最初のメンバーで最初の殉教者》

□ **summer** 名 夏

□ **sun** 名 《the –》太陽，日

□ **Sunita** 名 スニータ《不可触賤民の弟子の一人》

□ **support** 動 ①支える，支持する ②養う，援助する 名 ①支え，支持 ②援助，扶養

□ **suppose** 動 ①仮定する，推測する ②《be -d to ～》～することになっている，～するものである

□ **supreme** 形 最高の，究極の

□ **sure** 形 確かな，確実な，《be – to ～》必ず［きっと］～する，確信して

make sure 確かめる，確認する

□ **surely** 副 確かに，きっと

□ **surprised** 形 驚いた **be surprised to do** ～して驚く

□ **surprising** 形 驚くべき，意外な

□ **surrender** 動 降伏する，引き渡す

□ **swallow** 動 飲み込む

□ **swear** 動 ①誓う，断言する ②口汚くののしる

□ **sweet** 形 甘い

□ **sword** 名 剣，刀

□ **symbolize** 動 ①記号を用いる ②象徴する，象徴とみなす

□ **synagogue** 名 (ユダヤ教の) 礼拝堂，シナゴーグ

□ **Syria** 名 シリア《国名，地域名》

□ **table** 名 テーブル，食卓，台 **sit at the table** 食卓につく

T

□ **Taif** 名 ターイフ《サウジアラビアの都市》

□ **take** 動 ①取る，持つ ②持って［連れて］いく，捕らえる ③乗る ④(時間・労力を) 費やす，必要とする ⑤(ある動作を) する ⑥飲む ⑦耐える，受け入れる **take a look at** ～をちょっと見る **take a seat** 席にすわる **take care of** ～の世話をする，～の面倒を見る，～を管理する **take control of** ～を制御［管理］する，支配する **take from** ～から取られる **take hold of** ～をつかむ，捕らえる，制する **take off** (衣服を) 脱ぐ，取り去る，～を取り除く，離陸する，出発する **take one's place** (人と) 交代する，(人) の代わりをする，後任になる **take out** 取り出す，取り外す，連れ出す，持って帰る **take out of** ～から出す，～に連れ出す **take place** 行われる，起こる **take someone on a business trip** (人) を出張に連れて行く

169

□ **taken** 動 take (取る) の過去分詞

□ **Talitha Koum.** 「タリタ・クム (少女よ、起きなさい)」《アラム語》

□ **talk** 動 話す、語る、相談する 名 ①話、おしゃべり ②演説 ③《the −》話題

□ **Tapussa** 名 トラブサ、帝梨富婆《バクトリアから来た商人》

□ **task** 名 (やるべき) 仕事、職務、課題

□ **tathagata** 名 タターガタ、如来 (にょらい)《修行完成者 (悟りを開き、真理に達した者)》

□ **taught** 動 teach (教える) の過去、過去分詞

□ **tax** 名 税

□ **teach** 動 教える

□ **teacher** 名 先生、教師

□ **teaching** 動 teach (教える) の現在分詞 名 ①教えること、教授、授業 ②《-s》教え、教訓

□ **tear** 名 ①涙 ②裂け目 動 裂く、破る、引き離す

□ **teeth** 名 tooth (歯) の複数

□ **tell** 動 ①話す、言う、語る ②教える、知らせる、伝える ③わかる、見分ける **tell a lie** うそをつく **tell of** 〜について話す [説明する]

□ **temple** 名 寺、神殿

□ **tempt** 動 誘う、誘惑する、導く、心を引きつける

□ **ten** 名 10 (の数字)、10人 [個] 形 10の、10人 [個] の

□ **tent** 名 テント、天幕

□ **terrible** 形 恐ろしい、ひどい、ものすごい、つらい

□ **test** 動 試みる、試験する

□ **Thaddeus** 名 タダイ《十二使徒の一人》

□ **than** 接 〜よりも、〜以上に **more than** 〜以上 **rather than** 〜よりむしろ

□ **thank** 動 感謝する、礼を言う **thank 〜 for** 〜に対して礼を言う

□ **thankful** 形 ありがたく思う

□ **that** 形 その、あの **at that moment** その時に、その瞬間に **at that time** その時 代 ①それ、あれ、その [あの] 人 [物] ②《関係代名詞》〜である… 接 〜である、〜なので、〜だから **now that** 今や〜だから、〜からには **so that** 〜するために、それで、〜できるように **so 〜 that** … 非常に〜なので… 副 そんなに、それほど

□ **Thawr, the mountain of** サウル山《マッカの西南にある山》

□ **the** 冠 ①その、あの ②《形容詞の前で》〜な人々 副《− +比較級、− +比較級》〜すればするほど…

□ **their** 代 彼 (女) らの、それらの

□ **theirs** 代 彼 (女) らのもの、それらのもの

□ **them** 代 彼 (女) らを [に]、それらを [に]

□ **themselves** 代 彼 (女) ら自身、それら自身

□ **then** 副 その時 (に・は)、それから、次に 名 その時 **from then on** それ以来

□ **there** 副 ①そこに [で・の]、そこへ、あそこへ ②《− is [are] 〜》〜がある [いる] 名 そこ

□ **therefore** 副 したがって、それゆえ、その結果

□ **these** 代 これら、これ 形 これらの、この

□ **they** 代 ①彼 (女) らは [が]、それらは [が] ②《一般の》人は [が]

□ **thick** 形 厚い、密集した、濃厚な

□ **thief** 名 泥棒、強盗

□ **thieves** 名 thief (泥棒) の複数

□ **thigh** 名 太もも、大腿部

□ **thin** 形 薄い、細い、やせた、まばらな

□ **thing** 名 ①物、事 ②《-s》事情、事柄 ③《one's -s》持ち物、身の回り品

④ 人, やつ

□ **think** 動思う, 考える **think of** ～のことを考える, ～を思いつく, 考え出す

□ **third** 名第3 (の人 [物]) 形第3の, 3番の

□ **thirteen** 名13 (の数字), 13人 [個] 形13の, 13人 [個] の

□ **thirtieth** 形①《the –》30番目の ②30分の1 名①《the –》30番目 ②30分の1

□ **thirty** 名30 (の数字), 30人 [個] 形30の, 30人 [個] の

□ **this** 形①この, こちらの, これを ②今の, 現在の **in this way** このようにして **like this** このような, こんなふうに **this one** これ, こちら **this way** このように 代①これ, この人 [物] ②今, ここ

□ **Thomas** 名トマス《十二使徒の一人》

□ **thorn** 名とげ, とげのある植物, いばら

□ **those** 形それらの, あれらの **those who** ～する人々 代それら [あれら] の人 [物]

□ **though** 接①～にもかかわらず, ～だが ②たとえ～でも **even though** ～であるけれども, ～にもかかわらず 副しかし

□ **thought** 動think (思う) の過去, 過去分詞 名考え, 意見

□ **thoughtful** 形思慮深い, 考え込んだ

□ **thoughtfulness** 名思慮深さ

□ **thousand** 名①1000 (の数字), 1000人 [個] ②《– s》何千, 多数 形①1000の, 1000人 [個] の ②多数の

□ **threat** 名おどし, 脅迫

□ **threaten** 動脅かす, おびやかす, 脅迫する

□ **three** 名3 (の数字), 3人 [個] 形3の, 3人 [個] の

□ **threw** 動throw (投げる) の過去

□ **throat** 名のど, 気管

□ **through** 前～を通して, ～中を [に], ～中 副①通して ②終わりまで, まったく, すっかり **break through** ～を打ち破る **come through** 通り抜ける, 成功する, 期待に沿う **go through** 通り抜ける, 一つずつ順番に検討する **pass through** ～を通る, 通行する

□ **throughout** 前①～中, ～を通じて ②～のいたるところに 副初めから終わりまで, ずっと

□ **throw** 動投げる, 浴びせる

□ **thunder** 名雷, 雷鳴

□ **thus** 副①このように ②これだけ ③かくて, だから

□ **tightly** 副きつく, しっかり, 堅く

□ **time** 名①時, 時間, 歳月 ②時期 ③期間 ④時代 ⑤回, 倍 **a hard time** つらい時期 **all the time** ずっと, いつも, そのあいだずっと **any time** いつでも **at that time** その時 **at the time** そのころ, 当時は **by the time** ～する時までに **of the time** 当時の, 当節の **some time** いつか, そのうち **the last time** この前～したとき

□ **tiny** 形ちっぽけな, とても小さい

□ **tire** 動疲れる, 疲れさせる, あきる, あきさせる

□ **tired** 動tire (疲れる) の過去, 過去分詞 形①疲れた, くたびれた ②あきた, うんざりした

□ **to** 前①《方向・変化》～へ, ～に, ～の方へ ②《程度・時間》～まで ③《適合・付加・所属》～に ④《– + 動詞の原形》～するために [の], ～する, ～すること

□ **toe** 名足指, つま先

□ **together** 副①一緒に, ともに ②同時に **call together** 呼び集める, 集合する

□ **told** 動tell (話す) の過去, 過去分詞

□ **tongue** 名舌

□ **tonight** 名今夜, 今晩 副今夜は

□ **too** 副①～も (また) ②あまりに ～すぎる, とても～ **too much** 過度 の

□ **took** 動take (取る) の過去

□ **top** 名頂上, 首位

□ **tore** 動tear (裂く) の過去

□ **totally** 副全体的に, すっかり

□ **touch** 動触れる, さわる, ～を触れ させる

□ **tough-looking** 形強そうな外見 の, 屈強そうな

□ **towards** 前①《運動の方向・位置》 ～の方へ, ～に向かって ②《目的》 ～のために

□ **town** 名町, 都会, 都市

□ **trade** 名取引, 貿易, 商業

□ **trader** 名商人, 貿易業者

□ **trading** 名商取引

□ **traditional** 形伝統的な

□ **trap** 動わなを仕掛ける, わなで捕 らえる

□ **travel** 動①旅行する ②進む, 移動 する [させる]

□ **traveler** 名旅行者

□ **treat** 動扱う

□ **treatment** 名①取り扱い, 待遇 ②治療 (法)

□ **treaty** 名条約, 協定 **Treaty of Hudaybiyya** フダイビーヤの和議《ム ハンマドとマッカのクライシュ族の 間で結ばれた和議》

□ **tree** 名木, 樹木

□ **trench** 名①(深い) 溝, 排水溝, 堀 ②塹壕

□ **trial** 名①試み, 試験 ②苦難 ③裁 判

□ **tribe** 名部族, 一族

□ **trick** 名策略

□ **tried** 動try (試みる) の過去, 過去 分詞

□ **trip** 名(短い) 旅行, 遠征, 遠足, 出 張 **take someone on a business trip** (人) を出張に連れて行く

□ **trouble** 名①困難, 迷惑 ②心配, 苦労 ③もめごと **get into trouble** 面倒を起こす, 困った事になる, トラ ブルに巻き込まれた事になる **get into trouble with** ～とトラブルを起こす

□ **true** 形①本当の, 本物の, 真の ② 誠実な, 確かな **come true** 実現する

□ **truffle** 名トリュフ《キノコの一種》

□ **trust** 動信用 [信頼] する, 委託する 名信用, 信頼

□ **trustworthy** 形信用できる, あて になる

□ **truth** 名①真理, 事実, 本当 ②誠実, 忠実さ **four noble truths** 四諦 (し たい) または四聖諦 (ししょうたい) 《仏教が説く4種の基本的な真理。苦 諦 (この現実世界は苦であるという真 理), 集諦 (じったい。苦の原因は迷妄 と執着にあるという真理), 滅諦 (迷妄 を離れ, 執着を断ち切ることが, 悟り の境界にいたることであるという 真理), 道諦 (悟りの境界にいたる具 体的な実践方法は, 八正道であるとい う真理) のこと》

□ **try** 動①やってみる, 試みる ②努力 する, 努める **try one's best** 全力を 尽くす 名試み, 試し

□ **turmoil** 名動揺, 騒動, 混乱

□ **turn** 動①ひっくり返す, 回転する [させる], 曲がる, 曲げる, 向かう, 向 ける ②(～に) なる, (～に) 変える **turn around** 振り向く, 向きを変え る, 方向転換する **turn away** 向こう へ行く, 追い払う, (顔を) そむける, 横を向く **turn back** 元に戻る **turn into** ～に変わる **turn one's back on** ～に背中を向ける, ～を見捨てる **turn over** ひっくり返る [返す], (ペー ジを) めくる, 思いめぐらす, 引き 渡す **turn to** ～の方を向く, ～に頼 る, ～に変わる

□ **twelve** 名12 (の数字), 12人 [個]

形12の, 12人[個]の

□ **twenty** 图20(の数字), 20人[個]
形20の, 20人, 20[個]の

□ **two** 图2(の数字), 2人[個] 形2の,
2人[個]の

U

□ **Uddaka Ramputta** ウッダカ・
ラーマプッタ, 鬱頭藍弗 (うつらんほ
つ)《思想家。釈迦が出家後に師事し
た人物の1人》

□ **Uhud** 图ウフド山《マディーナの北
にある山》

□ **ultimate** 形最終の, 究極の

□ **Umar ibn al-Khattab** ウマル・
イブン・アル=ハッターブ《ムハンマ
ドの遠い親族》

□ **Umm Ayman** ウム・アイマン《ム
ハンマドの両親の召使で乳母の一人
だった女性》

□ **Umm Kulthum** 图ウンム・クル
スーム《ムハンマドの娘》

□ **umma** 图ウンマ, イスラム共同体
《イスラム教の信仰共同体のこと》

□ **uncle** 图おじ

□ **unclean** 形汚れた, 不浄の

□ **under** 前①《位置》~の下[に] ②
《状態》~で, ~を受けて, ~のもと
③《数量》~以下[未満]の, ~より下
の 副下に[で], 従属[服従]して

□ **understand** 動理解する, わかる,
~を聞いて知っている

□ **understanding** 图理解, 意見の
一致, 了解

□ **understood** 動understand (理解
する)の過去, 過去分詞

□ **unhappy** 形不運な, 不幸な

□ **unity** 图単一, 統一

□ **universe** 图《the – /the U-》宇宙,
全世界

□ **until** 前~まで(ずっと) 接~の時

まで, ~するまで

□ **unusual** 形普通でない, 珍しい,
見[聞き]慣れない

□ **up** 副①上へ, 上がって, 北へ ②立
って, 近づいて ③向上して, 増して
前①~の上(の方)へ, 高い方へ ②
(道)に沿って **blow up** 破裂する[さ
せる] **bring up** ①育てる, 連れて行
く ②(問題を)持ち出す **come up**
近づいてくる, 浮上する, 水面へ上っ
てくる **get up** 起き上がる, 立ち上が
る **give up** あきらめる, やめる, 引き
渡す **go up** ①~に上がる, 登る ②
~に近づく, 出かける ③(建物など
が)建つ, 立つ **go up to** ~まで行く,
近づく **grow up** 成長する, 大人にな
る **hold up** ~を持ち上げる **look
up** 見上げる, 調べる **look up to**
~を仰ぎ見る **make up for** 償う,
~の埋め合わせをする **open up** 広
がる, 広げる, 開く, 開ける **pick up**
拾い上げる **put up** ~を上げる, 揚げ
る, 建てる, 飾る **stand up** 立ち上が
る **wake up** (人を)起こす 形上向
きの, 上りの 图上昇, 向上, 値上がり

□ **upset** 形憤慨して, 動揺して 動気
を悪くさせる, (心・神経など)をかき
乱す

□ **us** 代私たちを[に]

□ **use** 動①使う, 用いる ②費やす
图使用, 用途

□ **used** 動①use (使う)の過去, 過去
分詞 ②《 – to》よく~したものだ, 以
前は~であった 形①慣れている,
《get [become] – to》~に慣れてくる
②使われた, 中古の

□ **usually** 副普通, いつも(は)

V

□ **Vaisakha** 图ヴァイサカ《ヒンド
ゥー暦の2番目の月》

□ **valley** 图谷, 谷間

□ **value** 動評価する, 値をつける, 大
切にする

- [ ] **Vaya dhamma sankhara, appamadena sampadetha.** 「諸行は無常である。不放逸に（怠ることなく）精進せよ」《釈迦の遺言と呼ばれる言葉》

- [ ] **Velama** 图 ヴェーラーマ《人名。偉大な布施をしていたバラモン》

- [ ] **verse** 图 詩, 詩の1行

- [ ] **very** 副 とても, 非常に, まったく

- [ ] **victim** 图 犠牲者, 被害者

- [ ] **victory** 图 勝利, 優勝

- [ ] **village** 图 村, 村落

- [ ] **vipassana** 图 ヴィパッサナー瞑想《今, この瞬間のありのままの現実（体と心）の変化を観察し続ける瞑想》

- [ ] **visit** 動 訪問する 图 訪問 **pay a visit** ～を訪問する

- [ ] **visitor** 图 訪問客

- [ ] **voice** 图 ①声, 音声 ②意見, 発言権

W

- [ ] **wait** 動 ①待つ,《– for ～》～を待つ ②延ばす, 延ばせる, 遅らせる ③《– on [upon] ～》～に仕える, 給仕をする

- [ ] **wake** 動 ①目がさめる, 起きる, 起こす ②奮起する **wake up** (人を)起こす

- [ ] **walk** 動 歩く, 歩かせる, 散歩する **walk around** 歩き回る, ぶらぶら歩く **walk away** 立ち去る, 遠ざかる **walk by** 通りかかる **walk on** 歩き続ける **walk over** ～の方に歩いていく

- [ ] **wall** 图 ①壁, 塀 ②障壁

- [ ] **want** 動 ほしい, 望む, ～したい, ～してほしい

- [ ] **war** 图 戦争 (状態), 闘争, 不和

- [ ] **Waraqa** ワラカ (・イブン・ナウファル)《ハディージャの従兄》

- [ ] **warm** 形 ①暖かい, 温暖な ②思いやりのある, 愛情のある

- [ ] **warn** 動 警告する, 用心させる

- [ ] **warrior** 图 戦士, 軍人

- [ ] **was** 動《be の第1・第3人称単数現在 am, is の過去》～であった, (～に)いた [あった]

- [ ] **wash** 動 洗う

- [ ] **waste** 图 浪費, 消耗

- [ ] **watch** 動 ①じっと見る, 見物する ②注意 [用心] する, 監視する

- [ ] **water** 图 ①水 ②(川・湖・海などの) 多量の水

- [ ] **wax** 图 ろう

- [ ] **way** 图 ①道, 通り道 ②方向, 距離 ③方法, 手段 ④習慣 **along the way** 途中で, これまでに, この先 **in a way** ある意味では **in this way** このようにして **on one's way** 途中で **on the way** 途中で **this way** このように **way of** ～する方法 **way out** 出口, 逃げ道, 脱出方法, 解決法 **way to** ～する方法

- [ ] **we** 代 私たちは [が]

- [ ] **weak** 形 ①弱い, 力のない, 病弱な ②劣った, へたな, 苦手な

- [ ] **weakly** 副 弱々しく

- [ ] **weakness** 图 ①弱さ, もろさ ②欠点, 弱点

- [ ] **wealth** 图 富, 財産

- [ ] **weapon** 图 武器, 兵器

- [ ] **wear** 動 着る, 着ている, 身につける

- [ ] **weather** 图 天気, 天候, 空模様

- [ ] **web** 图 クモの巣

- [ ] **wedding** 图 結婚式, 婚礼

- [ ] **week** 图 週, 1週間

- [ ] **weight** 图 重さ, 重力, 体重

- [ ] **welcome** 動 歓迎する

- [ ] **well** 副 ①うまく, 上手に ②十分に, よく, かなり **as well as** ～と同様に **be well -ed** よく [十分に] ～された

174

形健康な, 適当な, 申し分ない 名井戸

- **well-known** 形よく知られた, 有名な
- **went** 動 go (行く) の過去
- **wept** 動 weep (しくしく泣く) の過去, 過去分詞
- **were** 動《be の2人称単数・複数の過去》〜であった, (〜に) いた [あった]
- **what** 代①何が [を・に] ②《関係代名詞》〜するところのもの [こと] **what sort of** どういう **What's the matter?** どうしたんですか。 形①何の, どんな ②なんと ③〜するだけの 副いかに, どれほど
- **whatever** 代①《関係代名詞》〜するものは何でも ②どんなこと [もの] が〜とも 形①どんな〜でも ②《否定文・疑問文で》少しの〜も, 何らかの
- **when** 副①いつ ②《関係副詞》〜するところの, 〜するとその時, 〜するとき 接〜の時, 〜するとき 代いつ
- **whenever** 接①〜するときはいつでも, 〜するたびに ②いつ〜しても
- **where** 副①どこに [で] ②《関係副詞》〜するところの, そしてそこで, 〜するところ 接〜なところに [へ], 〜するところ [へ] 代①どこ, どの点 ②〜するところの
- **wherever** 接どこでも, どこへ [で] 〜するとも 副いったいどこへ [に・で]
- **whether** 接〜かどうか, 〜かまたは…, 〜であろうとなかろうと
- **which** 形①どちらの, どの, どれでも ②どんな〜でも, そしてこの 代①どちら, どれ, どの人 [物] ②《関係代名詞》〜するところの
- **while** 接①〜の間 (に), 〜する間 (に) ②一方, 〜なのに 名しばらくの間, 一定の時 **after a while** しばら

くして

- **whip** 名むち
- **whisper** 動ささやく, 小声で話す
- **white** 形①白い, (顔色などが) 青ざめた ②白人の 名白, 白色
- **who** 代①誰が [は], どの人 ②《関係代名詞》〜するところの (人) **those who** 〜する人々
- **whole** 形全体の, すべての, 完全な, 満一, 丸一 名《the –》全体, 全部
- **whom** 代①誰を [に] ②《関係代名詞》〜するところの人, そしてその人を
- **whose** 代①誰の ②《関係代名詞》(〜の) …するところの
- **why** 副①なぜ, どうして ②《関係副詞》〜するところの (理由) 間①おや, まあ ②もちろん, なんだって ③ええと
- **wide** 形幅の広い, 広範囲の, 幅が〜ある
- **widow** 名未亡人, やもめ
- **wield** 動巧みに使う, 扱う
- **wife** 名妻, 夫人
- **will** 動〜だろう, 〜しよう, する (つもりだ)
- **willing** 形①喜んで〜する, 〜しても構わない, いとわない ②自分から進んで行う
- **win** 動勝つ, 獲得する, 達する 名勝利, 成功
- **wind** 名①風 ②うねり, 一巻き
- **wine** 名ワイン, ぶどう酒
- **wing** 名翼, 羽
- **winter** 名冬
- **wipe** 動〜をふく, ぬぐう, ふきとる
- **wisdom** 名知恵, 賢明 (さ)
- **wise** 形賢明な, 聡明な, 博学の
- **wish** 動望む, 願う, (〜であればよいと) 思う

175

□ **with** 前①《同伴・付随・所属》~と一緒に，~を身につけて，~とともに②《様態》~（の状態）で，~して③《手段・道具》~で，~を使って **to begin with** はじめに，まず第一に **with all one's heart** 心から

□ **within** 前①~の中［内］に，~の内部に②~以内で，~を越えないで 副中［内］へ［に］，内部に

□ **without** 前~なしで，~がなく，~しないで

□ **wives** 名 wife（妻）の複数

□ **woke** 動 wake（目が覚める）の過去

□ **woman** 名（成人した）女性，婦人

□ **womb** 名 子宮

□ **women** 名 woman（女性）の複数

□ **won** 動 win（勝つ）の過去，過去分詞

□ **won't** will not の短縮形

□ **wonder** 動①不思議に思う，（~に）驚く②（~かしらと）思う **wonder if** ~ではないかと思う

□ **wonderful** 形 驚くべき，すばらしい，すてきな

□ **wood** 名①《しばしば-s》森，林②木材，まき

□ **word** 名①語，単語②ひと言

□ **wore** 動 wear（着ている）の過去

□ **work** 動①働く，勉強する，取り組む②機能［作用］する，うまくいく **work in** ~に入り込む **work of** ~の仕事 名①仕事，勉強②職③作品

□ **worker** 名 仕事をする人，労働者

□ **world** 名《the-》世界，~界 **in the world** 世界で

□ **worldly** 形 現世の，世俗的な

□ **worm** 名 虫，虫けらのような人

□ **worried** 形 心配そうな，不安げな **be worried about** （~のことで）心配している，~が気になる［かかる］

□ **worry** 動 悩む，悩ませる，心配する

［させる］**worry about** ~のことを心配する 名 苦労，心配

□ **worse** 形 いっそう悪い，より劣った，よりひどい

□ **worship** 動 崇拝する，礼拝［参拝］する，拝む

□ **worst** 形《the-》最も悪い，いちばんひどい，最も悪く，いちばんひどく《the-》最悪の事態［人・物］

□ **worthless** 形 価値のない，役立たずの

□ **worthy** 形 価値のある，立派な

□ **would** 助《will の過去》①~するだろう，~するつもりだ②~したものだ **Would you** ~？~してくださいませんか。 **would have … if** ~ もし~だったとしたら…しただろう **would like** ~がほしい

□ **wound** 名 傷

□ **writing** 名①書くこと，作文，著述②筆跡③書き物，書かれたもの，文書

□ **written** 動 write（書く）の過去分詞 形 文書の，書かれた

□ **wrong** 形①間違った，（道徳上）悪い②調子が悪い，故障した **be wrong with** （~にとって）よくない，~が故障している 副 間違って

Y

□ **Yashodhara** 名 ヤショーダラー，耶輸陀羅（やしゅだら）《釈迦の出家前の正妃》

□ **Yathrib** 名 ヤスリブ《町の名。のちにムハンマドによってマディーナと改名》

□ **year** 名①年，1年②学年，年度③~歳 **for ~ years** 何年も **for ~ years** ~年間，~年にわたって

□ **yellow** 形 黄色の 名 黄色

□ **yes** 副 はい，そうです 名 肯定の言葉［返事］

- [ ] **yet** 接 それにもかかわらず，しかし，けれども
- [ ] **you** 代 ①あなた(方)は[が]，あなた(方)を[に] ②(一般に)人は
- [ ] **young** 形 若い，幼い，青年の
- [ ] **your** 代 あなた(方)の
- [ ] **yours** 代 あなた(方)のもの
- [ ] **yourself** 代 あなた自身

Z

- [ ] **Zayd** 名 ザイド(・ビン・ハリタ)《元奴隷のイスラム教徒》
- [ ] **Zaynab** 名 ザイナブ《ムハンマドの娘》

A
B
C
D
E
F
G
H
I
J
K
L
M
N
O
P
Q
R
S
T
U
V
W
X
Y
Z

English Conversational Ability Test
国際英語会話能力検定

● E-CATとは…
英語が話せるようになるための
テストです。インターネット
ベースで、30分であなたの発
話力をチェックします。

www.ecatexam.com

● iTEP®とは…
世界各国の企業、政府機関、アメリカの大学
300校以上が、英語能力判定テストとして採用。
オンラインによる90分のテストで文法、リー
ディング、リスニング、ライティング、スピー
キングの5技能をスコア化。iTEP®は、留学、就
職、海外赴任などに必要な、世界に通用する英
語力を総合的に評価する画期的なテストです。

www.itepexamjapan.com

ラダーシリーズ
Three Religious Leaders: Jesus, Buddha, and Muhammad
イエス／ブッダ／ムハンマド―世界三大宗教の開祖たち

2021年11月1日　第1刷発行

著　者　アラン・ムーア＆ギル・タヴナー
　　　　R・N・ピライ
　　　　アムド・アボ・ネガー

発行者　浦　晋亮

発行所　IBCパブリッシング株式会社
　　　　〒162-0804 東京都新宿区中里町29番3号
　　　　菱秀神楽坂ビル9F
　　　　Tel. 03-3513-4511　Fax. 03-3513-4512
　　　　www.ibcpub.co.jp

印　刷　株式会社シナノパブリッシングプレス
装　丁　伊藤 理恵
編集協力　Ed Jacob

Printed in Japan
ISBN978-4-7946-0682-2